Natural Gas & Electric Power
in Nontechnical Language

by Ann Chambers

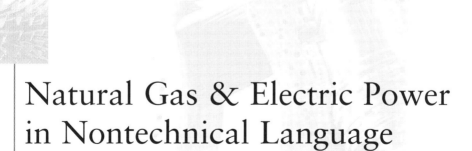

Natural Gas & Electric Power
in Nontechnical Language

by Ann Chambers

PennWell Books
PennWell Publishing Company
Tulsa, Oklahoma

Copyright 1999 by
PennWell
1421 S. Sheridan Road/P.O. Box 1260
Tulsa, Oklahoma 74101

Library of Congress Cataloging-in-Publication Data
    Chambers, Ann.
        Natural Gas & Electric Power in Nontechnical Language /
        by Ann Chambers
            p. cm.
            Includes index
            ISBN 0-87814-761-6
               1. Electric power-plants-- United States--Fuel--Popular works.
    2. Gas as fuel--Popular works. 3. Gas power plants--United
    States--Poplar works. 4. Gas industry--United States--Popular
    works. 5. Electric utilities-- United States--Popular works. I. Title.
    TK1061.C49   1999
    621.31--dc21   99-13897
                                             CIP

Printed in the United States of America.

Contents

Tables

Figures

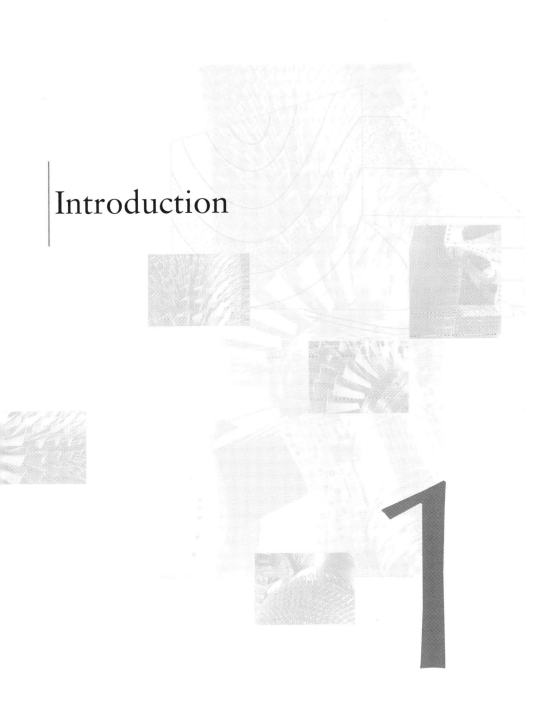

Introduction

1

n atural gas is an important element in our nation's energy mix—one that is expected to grow in importance in the new millennium. It is the fuel of choice in the electric power industry, with almost all the new construction designed to burn it.

The electric industry is going through a painful deregulation process, restructuring itself and jockeying for strength in the open market to come. Impending deregulation stifled generation construction throughout the country for several years, as utilities waited and watched. They were afraid to spend money on new construction, because it was uncertain whether those expenditures would be recouped. Meanwhile excess capacity fell from around 17% to dangerously low levels. Rolling blackouts during peak summer usage pointed out in no uncertain terms that something needed to be done.

Finally in the late 1990s, as the course of deregulation became somewhat established, excess capacity shortages almost ensured the profitability of new generation in the deregulated market, and a construction boom was born. One of the primary beneficiaries of this construction boom is the natural gas industry.

Natural gas has already been through deregulation, and the firms that survived it see enormous profit potential in the deregulation of the electric industry. Gas companies and electric utilities began building new generation facilities, almost all of them powered by natural gas.

The natural gas used in the U.S. is primarily produced here, so few import-export issues muddy the waters. Overseas politics will not affect supply. Domestic natural gas production accounts for 86% of the gas used in the U.S., with the majority of the imports coming from Canada. Domestic production is expected to increase from 19 trillion cubic feet today to more than 26 trillion cubic feet by 2015—enough growth to allow domestic production to continue accounting for 86% of our gas.

In addition, natural gas prices have fallen in line with the prices of the other fossil fuels, which are the primary fuels of electricity production. Nuclear energy is the only non-fossil fuel driving a significant percentage of our electricity generating capacity. With our abundant resources of gas and ever-developing technology for finding and producing it, gas prices are expected to remain low, at least through the next couple of decades.

Coal, while inexpensive and domestically abundant, is viewed as dirty. As emissions regulations increase and tighten, coal-burning utilities must add expensive scrubbing equipment to meet emissions standards, driving up the cost of their electricity. The uncertainty of future emissions demands and the expense of this additional equipment are stalling coal-fired construction. Oil-fired construction is basically non-existent for similar reasons. But natural gas has the least emissions worries of all the fossil fuels. It is viewed as a clean fuel, adding to its popularity. Natural gas-fired capacity is also faster and cheaper to build than many other types of plants.

According to forecasts from the American Gas Association, natural gas consumption is expected to increase by more than 40% by 2015, fueled by strong industrial demand, the popularity of gas among new-home buyers and commercial customers—and a significant load increase from new gas-fired electricity generation facilities. That amount of growth will bring the natural gas share of the U.S. energy market to more than 28%.

Total U.S. natural gas consumption is expected to rise from about 23 quadrillion Btu in 1997 to 32 quadrillion Btu in 2015. The strongest growth is expected to take place in the electric utility sector, where the economic and environmental benefits of gas-fired generation will allow gas to continue capturing the lion's share of the market for new generating capacity. Electric utilities are expected to more than double their consumption of natural gas between 1998 and 2015. Electricity generation used 2.9 quadrillion Btu in 1997, and it is expected to consume close to 7.0 quadrillion Btu by 2015.

Merchant power—a relatively new phenomenon in the U.S. electricity market—is relying almost exclusively on natural gas for fuel. One reason is that natural gas companies are often building these facilities. These firms, and electric utilities that see potential to maximize their profits in an open market through diversification and control of their fuel supplies, are driving the convergence of these two massive industries.

The electric power industry accounts for $200 billion annually, and the natural gas industry exceeds $80 billion annually, so they are both major industries here in the U.S. However, together they are creating a new $300 billion Btu industry, and the effects of that cannot be overestimated.

In this book, we will take a look at the history of these two converging industries and the forces that are pressing them together—political, regulatory, technical, and economic. The basics of gas—including exploration, drilling, production, transportation, and trading—are all explained in easy-to-understand language. We will also discuss other fuels competing for market share in the electric industry, the merchant plant uprising, the growing popularity of distributed generation, and strategies for creating value in the new Btu stream.

Natural Gas History

1

n atural gas was used in the U.S. as early as 1821, but it was not until the 1920s that it began to capture a share of the energy market. Until then, the discovery of natural gas was more frequently an unwelcome event, especially for coal miners who dreaded the explosive vapor. Colonel Drake's first oil well drilled in Pennsylvania in 1859 ushered in the petroleum era, but common use of natural gas was more than a half century away.

Gas provided the lift for oil surging from Drake's well, and the oil field furnished gas for the continent's first successful natural gas transport system built in 1872. Wrought iron pipe, two inches in diameter, spanned more than five miles from the well to a nearby village. An important breakthrough in the transportation of natural gas came in 1890, with S.R. Dresser's invention of a leakproof coupling. Pipeline construction remained cumbersome however, and no one moved gas more than about 100 miles from its source.

Gas was an unreliable product back then, as there was no way to tell whether a well would continue producing or quickly run dry. Gas wells carried enormous economic risk. Meanwhile coal and oil were cheap, so there was little economic incentive to overcome the difficulties associated with natural gas.

Manufactured gas and lighting

From its discovery in the 19th century, gas was used almost exclusively as a source of light. It wasn't until the early 20th century that electricity took over the lighting market. At that time gas companies shifted their efforts to thermal uses, such as gas appliances, including water heaters, air conditioners, and cook stoves.

In the last century, gas was produced from coal in "gas works" located in urban areas. Usually, the same company that manufactured the gas operated the pipelines and distribution system. Today, few gas producers are involved in long-distance transmission or urban distribution. Industrial and electric utility markets for this "manufactured" gas were relatively small until after World War II, when natural gas became widely available. Before then, the gas industry marketed manufactured gas to illuminate streets and homes. Gas manufactured from coal was practical for lighting, but it made no economic sense to burn expensive manufactured gas in boilers, which could run on inexpensive coal.

Gas works that appeared throughout the U.S. beginning in the 1920s soon displaced tallow candles as the main source of residential lighting. Manufactured gas was able to charge a price commensurate with its cost because its flame was far better than anything else available. Whale oil was its strongest competitor until over-hunting brought the whaling era to an end. In the 1870s, a new competitor captured a large share of the lighting market, when kerosene displayed its advantages—it posed little danger of asphyxiation, did not require pipelines, and burned with a brighter flame.

The Wellsbach mantle lamp hit the market in 1885, boosting the popularity of manufactured gas as a light source because the incandescent lamp improved the lighting characteristics of gas sevenfold. Then, in 1892, Thomas Edison started the first central electricity generator in New York City, ending the reign of manufactured-gas lighting with startling speed.

From light to heat

The transition of gas from an illuminant to a heat source caused a revolution in measuring standards. Originally, the energy value of gas was expressed in *candlepower*. The conversion to a heat standard began in 1908 when the Wisconsin Public Utilities Commission ordered gas distributors to use *British thermal units* (Btu).

The home heating and appliance market for gas was limited until manufactured gas was replaced by non-toxic, cheap, and abundant supplies of natural gas. Chicago led the way, when in 1931, gas distributor Peoples Gas Light and Coke Company connected Chicago to the world's largest gas producing area of the time—the fields of southwestern Kansas. By the end of World War II, the gas industry was flourishing. For the next 30 years, homeowners and industries in the U.S. enjoyed inexpensive natural gas.

Pipelines and Transport

Until the pipeline boom that followed World War II, natural gas produced in association with oil exploration was mostly flared or vented. Until recently, gaseous fuels were far more difficult and costly to move than solid coal and liquid oil. Liquid and solid fuels can be poured or scooped into barrels, bins, or tanks and carried to market by highway, rail, or sea. But the most efficient way to transport gas is through fixed, high-pressure pipes.

Pipes are not necessarily a disadvantage. The problem was that the technology was not yet available to make them affordable. Today, pipelines are the preferred mode for overland shipments of oil and slurry pipelines are one of the cheapest ways to move large volumes of semi-liquefied coal.

Improvements in pipeline technology were erratic. The first gas pipeline to span more than 100 miles ran to Chicago from gas fields in Indiana; it was built in 1891. It carried gas 120 miles without compressors. The gas happened to come out of the ground at a pressure high enough to ensure an acceptable rate of flow. The amount of gas a pipeline can deliver depends on its diameter and the horsepower and spacing of its compressor stations. Today's trunklines operate at pressures in the range of 1,000 psi with pressure boost every 100 or 200 miles. The Chicago pipeline gas from 1891 came out of the ground at 525 psi. Compressors were in use as early as 1880, but compressors were not the limiting factor to pipeline growth. The quality of the pipe was a more significant handicap. Pipeline industry development depended on strengthening pipe seams, couplings, and steel to withstand the high pressures needed.

Safety was also an issue. Unlike liquids, gases can be compressed almost without limit, and they can then later be expanded back to atmospheric pressure. A small hole or crack in an oil pipeline can be troublesome, but it is far less dangerous than a hole in a high-pressure gas pipeline. A small flaw can cause a catastrophic failure. As time passed, steel pipe began to replace cast-iron. Even then, the strength of pipe was compromised by its being rolled from flat sections and joined by rivets or bolts. Thicker walls did not improve the pipe's ability to withstand high pressures because the seams were still weak.

Seam-sealing and pipe-joining techniques advanced in 1911 when oxy-acetylene welding was introduced. It was followed by electric welding in 1922. Pressure-gas welding used during and after World War II, combined with manufacturing breakthroughs that cut the costs of steel, paved the way for the pipeline construction boom.

As technologies continued to improve, the industry used ever-increasing pipe diameters and pressures, which boosted system capacities and economies of scale (Table 1-1).

Long-distance gas transmission became practical in the late 1920s, and between 1927 and 1931, about a dozen major transmission systems emerged, each with pipelines covering distances exceeding 200 miles. These systems used gas from three hydrocarbon provinces: the Panhandle-Hugoton fields; the Monroe field in Louisiana, and California's San Joaquin Valley. The Panhandle fields are the biggest single accumulation of gas in the Western

Table 1-1. Pipeline Capacity Growth

Year	Max. Pipe Diameter	Design Pressures
1930	20"	500 psig
1950	26"	800 psig
1960	36"	1,000 psig
1975	42"	1,260 psig

Although some pipelines have been planned at up to 56-inch diameter pipe, the pipeline diameters in use seem to have peaked in the 42-inch range. Pressure in the table is noted in pounds per square inch, gauge (psig), which is pounds per square inch minus the 14.7 psi from atmospheric pressure.

Hemisphere. They stretch almost 300 miles from the northern part of the Texas Panhandle, across Oklahoma, and into southwestern Kansas.

The Great Depression stalled the growth of the natural gas industry as pipeline construction came to a standstill between 1932 and the U.S. entry into WWII. The war stimulated energy consumption in East Coast industrial centers but enemy submarines made it risky to move oil by tanker—many of which were sunk off the U.S. coast. In response, the federal government granted the Tennessee Gas Transmission Company special privileges to gather labor and steel for a 1,275 mile pipeline running from the Gulf Coast to the Appalachians. The government also built oil pipelines from fields in Texas to the upper Midwest and the Appalachians for national defense purposes. After the war, these lines were converted to natural gas.

Rationing of consumer appliances and industrial steel ended with the war, and a frenzy of pipeline construction began that lasted until the mid 1960s. The Panhandle and Hugoton fields continued to support new pipeline growth and companies expanded systems with more compressors. Attention also turned to Texas and the Carthage gas field, discovered in the 1930s. Successful wildcats were drilled on the Texas and Louisiana Gulf

Coast. This region accounts for about 40% of all U.S. natural gas discovered to date. Between 1950 and 1956, five pipelines, each exceeding a thousand miles, were built from the Gulf Coast to destinations in the north and east.

In 1953, Permian Basin gas began flowing north and east for the first time. Northern Natural pioneered the connection, reversing the flow of a pipeline that had previously carried Panhandle gas southward into western Texas.

The postwar boom was still in full swing in the late 1950s as interstate transmission companies augmented their systems, boosting capacity to accommodate growth in existing markets. A few new routes were established to add markets, as well. Gas came to Florida in 1959 when the Houston Corp. built more than 1,500 miles of mainline from the tip of Texas to Miami, Florida. Lateral lines distributed gas throughout the state.

By the mid 1960s, the postwar pipeline boom had ended. Transcontinental construction was succeeded by less dramatic projects that brought the U.S. gas transmission network to maturity. By 1966, natural gas was available to consumers in every state but Hawaii, and to all but the Maritime provinces of Canada. Overall, the industry was relatively stagnant in the 1960s.

Throughout the 1970s, federal regulation of the industry fostered shortages, curtailments, and pessimism about future supply. This pessimism persisted through the 1980s, based on stubbornly stagnant demand and lingering doubt about adequate long-term supply. Sales to residential, commercial, and industrial customers remained below the 1972 peak of 17.1 billion Btu for 19 years, reaching 17.3 Btu and breaking the record in 1991.

By the mid 1990s natural gas had been largely deregulated, and its popularity skyrocketed. Natural gas—long seen as a clean, inexpensive, reliable fuel—was launched into rapid growth that is expected to continue for the next couple of decades.

Regulation

As the natural gas transportation network developed throughout the country, so did the web of federal regulation. One regulatory step followed another, and over a period of nearly four decades, the government's grip on the industry broadened and tightened. Toward the end of that four-decade span, regulators and lawmakers realized that the problem was not in the details of regulation, but in the regulation itself.

Gas regulation started as franchising of companies granted exclusive rights to manufacture and distribute gas from coal in a single city. It evolved, however, into tariff regulation for pipelines that crossed state lines, and then into controls of prices at wellhead and fuel choices at the point of consumption. Gas producers protested and lobbied, but to no avail. In retrospect it is clear that regulation was bad for natural gas as a fuel and for the entities that produce or use it. Price controls discouraged development of gas reserves and artificial incentives brought forward otherwise uneconomic supply. During several extreme winters in the 1970s, the regulated interstate market experienced shortages while the unregulated intrastate market was awash in gas. The economy paid for these inefficiencies.

The Natural Gas Act (NGA) of 1938, the Natural Gas Policy Act (NGPA) of 1978, the Outer Continental Shelf Lands Act (OCSLA), the Natural Gas Wellhead Decontrol Act (NGWDA) of 1989, and the Energy Policy Act (EPA) of 1992 are the primary laws the Federal Energy Regulatory Commission (FERC) administers to oversee America's natural gas pipeline industry. (See "Key Dates" at the end of this chapter.)

Deregulation

Prior to 1985, regulated interstate gas pipelines operated much like today's electric industry: pipelines provided a bundled service to customers that included transportation, transportation-related services such as storage, and the gas commodity.

Unlike electric utilities, pipelines did not generally produce the commodity. Instead, they bought it from unaffiliated gas producers under long-term contracts at regulated prices. Customers paid the cost of gas under these contracts on a pass-through basis in their rates. That is—unlike electric utilities, which earn a return on the commodity they generate and include it in their rates—pipelines made no profit on the purchase and sale of gas.

In the mid 1980s, pipelines' contractual commitments to buy large amounts of gas at escalating regulated prices for decades into the future—the costs of which would flow through to the customers—were much like the high-cost generation capacity in the rate bases of many of today's electric utilities.

Prompted by service curtailments resulting from shortages in the 1970s, and projections of future oil prices exceeding $100/bbl, pipelines contracted for large volumes of long-term gas supplies under high incentive prices provided by the Natural Gas Policy Act of 1978 (NGPA). By the mid 1980s, things had changed. The gas shortage had disappeared, oil prices had stalled well short of $100/bbl, and industrial customers who could switch from gas to oil or other fuels were doing so. Yet, despite weakening gas markets, resale rates regulated by the Federal Energy Regulatory Commission (FERC) continued to rise. The problem was the high-cost gas commitments dated in the late 1970s and early 1980s. As market prices for gas declined, the production from older, low-priced supply sources fell while the volume of high-priced gas under contract was rising. Under cost-of-service rules—which made the average cost of all gas purchased a pass-through item in resale rates—customers were seeing higher and higher rates.

In most cases, this increase in the volume of high-cost supplies did not result from a failure on the part of pipeline supply managers to recognize or react to changing market conditions. Many high-cost, post-NGPA contracts bound the pipeline to buy all that the producer chose to deliver from his reserves. Of course, with energy prices falling generally, and pipeline contracts providing for price escalation, producers made every effort to develop and produce existing reserves while these contracts were in force. As a result, post-NGPA gas supplies with escalating prices assumed a larger and larger role in most pipelines' supply portfolios. It was a stranded cost problem, although at the time the contracts were discussed as a prudence issue. Even when market conditions had changed, creating an opportunity for substantial gas cost savings, past contractual arrangements approved—many would say prompted—by regulators had locked in prices based upon an energy-crisis mentality of prior years, and consumers were seeing no savings.

There were several options for dealing with the problem. FERC could have declared prices under the high-priced contracts imprudent, preventing further pass-through of the premium above current market. This would have left pipelines and producers to decide who should absorb the loss under the contracts. FERC could have decided that competitive wellhead gas markets would afford customers the best opportunities and the best protections and, on that basis, deregulated the commodity side of the gas business (which it did with FERC Order 636). Premiums over marketing in existing gas contracts would then have been stranded by lower-priced, competitively available supplies. FERC initially did neither.

Instead, FERC identified the problem as being one of poorly functioning market signals. FERC found that current gas market values were not having their full effect on pipeline or customer gas purchase decisions. To solve that problem, FERC took steps to make the consequences of ignoring market signals more severe.

In 1984, FERC issued Order 380, outlawing contractual provisions under which customers had agreed to pay for contractually committed supplies even if they did not actually take delivery. Pipeline customers suddenly had the freedom to seek out low-cost supplies and avoid paying for high-cost gas from old contracts.

In 1985, FERC issued Order 436, which required pipelines desiring to provide transportation service to the expanding market of direct purchasers to give their existing sales customers the option of converting to service under equally favorable terms. In concept then, regulated pipeline suppliers—still selling gas under old rates—would coexist with unregulated competitive gas sellers who would contract for transportation service from the same pipelines with whom they competed.

But the concept did not work. By prohibiting the collection of gas costs in non-volumetric tariffs, FERC gave gas customers a free ride on their traditional suppliers. The merchant services involved costs that did not relate to volumes actually taken.

Over the next decade, a host of new merchant and transmission rate design proposals emerged to solve the many problems under the system. These included gas inventory charges, deficiency charges, zone transmission rates, market/production area rates, and telescoping rates.

In many cases, the deregulation process took the form of horse-trading. A regulated pipeline supplier would propose initiatives to get customers to take responsibility for outstanding obligations under existing supply contracts in exchange for expanded transmission service options for better access and more competitive choices for supplies. None of this worked. The FERC would not approve pipeline proposals to charge customers for maintaining stand-by supplies which the customer didn't take. Third parties would not compete directly with pipelines because the FERC would not approve tariffs for pipelines that reflected true costs. Customers would not relinquish their entitlement to free stand-by service until there were established third-party providers of the same commodity service.

Nearly 10 years after the onset of the problem, the FERC finally resorted to divestiture. The merchant function was removed from the pipelines and left to contractual dealings between customers and unregulated suppliers and merchants. The merchant side of the business was deregulated effectively.

It is commonly believed that the advent of competition saved natural gas customers tens of billions of dollars. However, many in the industry say that supposition does not hold up. Average wholesale prices for natural gas before and after restructuring, and the price savings, come primarily through the decrease in price of gas, not the margin charged on it. This suggests that buyers of gas at wholesale did not save money as a result of added competition. The premise behind merchant deregulation was that well-head gas markets were already competitive. If competition created by deregulation did lower prices, it would have done so by reducing the margin paid to merchants, and that did not happen.

The multi-billion dollar estimates of customer savings are typically calculated by comparing gas commodity costs as they are now with estimates of where they would have been, had gas supply contracts of the early 1980s been fully performed. Energy markets generally saw larger real price declines during the 1980s than in any post-war decade. Those declines are reflected in today's commodity prices. Old NGPA contracts, if they had been left in place, probably would have caused commodity rates to rise. This assumption is the basis of the estimated savings through deregulation. But the real reason for those savings is that high-cost gas contracts were reformed or terminated during deregulation—not through competition.

Widespread contract reform and terminations occurred. The FERC let customers who were otherwise bound to buy the high-priced gas under their service agreements reduce purchases without making contractually required minimum bill payments. The FERC also made sure, through open-access rules, that customers who rejected their high-priced supplies would find cheap spot gas to take its place. Finally, the FERC was careful not to make any commitments concerning the ability of pipelines to recover costs associated with supply contracts where customers failed to purchase the volumes pipelines were committed to take.

These things together forced pipelines and producers to absorb the stranded costs associated with older, high-priced contracts. More than 80% of the total settlement cost—estimated at $40 billion in contract relief—was paid by producers and pipelines. The risk of leaving old contracts in place and accumulating continuing liabilities as customers chose to buy gas elsewhere was just too great.

In the new market, buyers could purchase gas solely as a commodity at a commodity-only price. They could still get other aspects of the traditional merchant service, when needed, by purchasing limited volumes from the contractually bound pipeline supplier. In the end, rather than competing with each other, pipelines and other marketers complemented one another. Pipelines provided peak-day reliability and marketers provided the commodity. Marketers and direct purchasers flourished because pipelines gave gas customers a free ride on other necessary services.

The wellhead price of natural gas increased only slightly in the decade from 1987 to 1996. In 1987, gas cost $2.21 per thousand cubic feet and in 1996, it cost $2.24 per thousand cubic feet. According to the American Gas Association (AGA), transmission and distribution costs for gas dropped from $2.20 to $1.40 per thousand cubic feet. Retail natural gas prices for all sectors fell 18% between 1987 and 1996.

The gas companies are maintaining their core businesses, but they are also working aggressively to expand their businesses in non-regulated markets. Unregulated subsidiaries can compete in other markets, selling different forms of energy and energy products and services.

Key Dates in Natural Gas Deregulation

1978 The Natural Gas Policy Act (NGPA) ends federal control of the wellhead price of gas as of Jan. 1, 1985, but maintains wellhead price control for older vintages of gas.

1985 Federal Energy Regulatory Commission (FERC) Order 436 establishes a voluntary program that encourages natural gas pipelines to open access to carriers of natural gas bought by users from producers.

1989 Natural Gas Wellhead Decontrol Act (NGWDA) lifts all remaining wellhead price controls.

1992 FERC Order 636 orders interstate natural gas pipelines to unbundle gas sales, transportation, and storage.

1995 The first residential natural gas customer choice programs are implemented. By 1997, local natural gas utilities in 17 states and the District of Columbia had proposed or implemented residential customer choice or pilot programs.

1996   FERC issues Order 888 promoting wholesale competition through open access, non-discriminatory transmission services by public utilities; recovery of stranded costs by public utilities and transmitting utilities. Also in 1996, FERC issued Order 889 mandating open access to same-time information systems and standards of conduct.

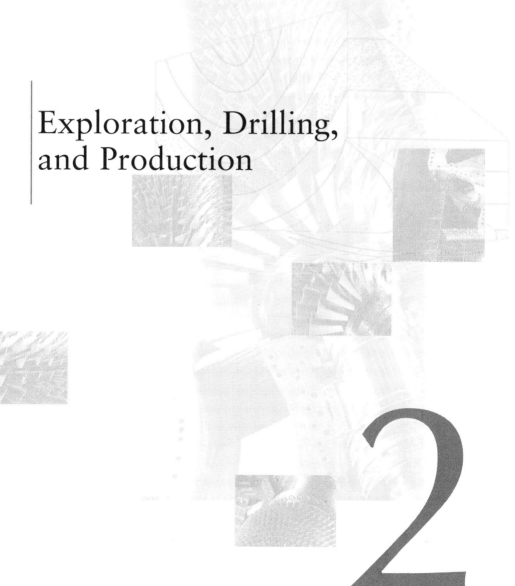

Exploration, Drilling, and Production

2

P
etroleum products, including natural gas, come from the decomposed remains of ancient plants and animals. Erosion carries biological remains down rivers and streams onto shorelines, where they rest with mud and silt. Over time, the remains, covered by sediment, are compressed by the weight of sedimentary layers forming over them. With time, pressure, and heat, the material forms sedimentary rock. Today, petroleum products are often found in formations of sedimentary rocks such as sandstone, shale, and dolomite.

Oil and gas move through the pores of the sedimentary rock, upward toward the surface. If gas or light oils reach the surface they will evaporate. Most petroleum never makes it to the surface. The products will become trapped beneath the surface by layers of rock that have formed above the sedimentary rock layers that produced the petroleum.

Rocks that trap petroleum deposits are impermeable layers generally shaped into domes by folding or faults. The layer that traps the gas and oil is called a *cap rock* and the formation is called a *trap* (Fig. 2-1).

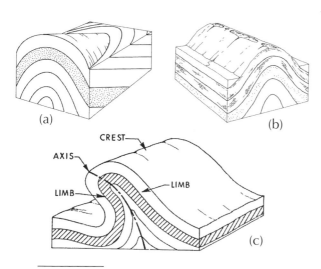

Fig. 2-1. Examples of Rock Formations that can hold Petroleum Deposits

(a, b) An anticline, a large upward arch of sedimentary rocks, deformed by folding. A large downward arch of rock is called a syncline. A circular or elliptical uplift is called a dome. (c) The parts of a fold.

Exploration

In the early days of petroleum exploration, people looked at the surface of the earth for evidence of a formation likely to contain oil. Oil wells were often dug based primarily on intuition rather than science.

Geologists now conduct tests to determine the likelihood of gas and oil deposits. They study ground rock formations to determine where rock layers are folded to create traps. Technology has also advanced to help determine the location of underground petroleum. *Seismology*—the study of how sound waves move through the earth's crust—is an invaluable tool for geologists. Vibrations are affected differently by different kinds of rock, so recording how a layer of rock reflects sound waves gives the geologist an educated guess about the type of rock and its depth. Computer technology

*Fig. 2-2. Major Gas
Producing Sedimentary
Basins of North America*

has aided seismology, bringing 3-D seismic data to the field. This creates a three-dimensional map of the rock layers beneath the surface using thousands of seismic measurements. The data are entered into a computer for analysis and creation of the 3-D model. With traditional techniques, the chances of finding petroleum when drilling a well range are between 10% and 20%. With 3-D seismology, the odds are considerably increased. However, even with all of today's technology, the only way to be sure whether a gas or oil deposit lies under a specific site is to drill a well.

North America has abundant natural gas reserves, sited in several major basins (Fig. 2-2). Proved reserves in the U.S. sit at 4.7 trillion cubic meters of gas, while Canada has 1.9 trillion cubic meters and Mexico adds another 1.9 trillion cubic meters, for a North American total of 8.5 trillion cubic meters. Total world proven reserves exceed 145 trillion cubic meters (Table 2-1).

Table 2-1 Proved Reserves of Natural Gas, 1997

In trillion cubic meters	
U.S.	4.7
Canada	1.9
Mexico	1.9
Total North America	8.5
Total World	145

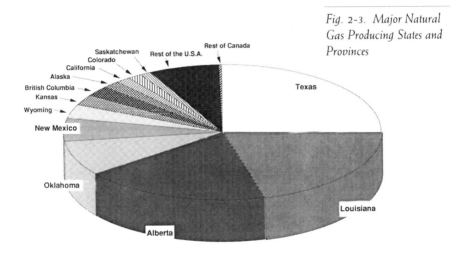

Fig. 2-3. Major Natural Gas Producing States and Provinces

Much of the North American natural gas production comes from a handful of states and provinces, most notably Texas, Louisiana, Alberta, Oklahoma, and New Mexico (Fig. 2-3).

Drilling

Once a promising site is located, the location will determine the types of equipment needed to drill the well. If the formation is expected to be relatively shallow, a cable drilling rig may be used. Deeper formations require the use of rotary drilling rigs. The nature of the rock formation is also a factor in choosing drilling equipment.

Percussion—or cable-tool drilling—involves repeatedly raising and dropping a metal bit into the hole. Loose soils and rock chips must be periodically removed from the hole to give the bit a clear shot at the bottom of the well. Steel pipe is used to keep the sides of the well from collapsing.

Rotary drilling differs from percussion in that it relies on a sharp bit to drill through earth and rock layers. The bit is also used to lift waste materials out of the well. A complex system of cables, engines, support mechanisms, lubricating devices, and pulleys, control the bit and keep it lubricated. Under the surface, the bit is attached to a long drill pipe. There are a variety of different types of bits for drilling through different conditions and rock types. For a deep well drilled through several types of rock, several different types of bits may be needed.

Drilling fluids are also important in rotary drilling. The fluids are used to cool the bit, remove debris, and coat the wellbore. Most drilling fluids have a clay base customized for the specific formations being drilled. The fluids form a cake on the walls of the drill hole that helps prevent collapse of the well until steel casing can be installed.

Technological advances have helped companies cut costs while increasing the value of wells. One of the most dramatic technologies is horizontal drilling. Wells that are not vertical to the surface are not a new phenomenon. Slant drilling has been used for many years to drill wells at an angle to reach areas where rigs could not be placed. Slant drilling has been used in offshore drilling where it can reduce the number of expensive platforms needed. In some cases 20 or more slanted wells can be drilled from one platform. Horizontal drilling makes a 90° turn after only a few feet. There are many benefits to horizontal drilling. A horizontal well can penetrate more than one reservoir and can produce up to six or seven times as much gas as an equivalent vertical well.

Salt-water production is reduced. The life of a well can be increased from 25% of the product to more than 50%. Oil and gas can be extracted as drilling continues.

Offshore drilling

Offshore drilling has been practiced since 1869. Early offshore rigs were sited in shallow water. Offshore drilling surged after World War II when the technology became available to make these efforts profitable.

The primary difference between onshore and offshore drilling is siting. For drilling on land, the land provides the base for the rig, whereas in offshore wells, the base is man-made. In offshore wells, the floating drilling platform is first attached to the base of ocean, while allowing for waves and movement on the surface. To do this, an underwater base is moved into position and a hole about 100 feet deep is drilled into the ocean floor. The shallow hole is filled with a casting to serve as a permanent base for the drilling template. The template is a box with several large round holes in it. It is used as a guide for several wells. Other equipment is then attached to the template.

There are several types of platforms that can be attached to this drilling base, depending on the depth of the water, distance from the shoreline and the strength of waves. A barge can be used as a platform when drilling near shore, while larger rigs are needed for wells that are far from shore, in open ocean, or over very deep water. Once these large platforms are in place over the drilling site, their base is filled with water so they sit on the water. They are held in place with weights and anchor cables. Drilling ships, which look like regular ships but have a drilling platform in their hull, can also be used in deep waters.

Permanent offshore drilling platforms are placed in areas where multiple wells will be drilled, with anticipated high production levels over the long term. The platforms built for projects in the North Sea are some of the largest structures ever built. They sit on 500 feet of water. They are quite strong—able to take waves more than 60 feet high and winds exceeding 90 knots. Platforms may be more than 450 feet in diameter and weigh more than 550,000 tons.

Production

Once gas is found, a variety of tests are run to determine the most efficient recovery rate, based on the fastest rate that gas can be removed without harming the formation. Other tests check pressure, heat and other variables in the well. Some wells have enough natural pressure that the gas will flow without need for a pump or lifting system. These are rare, and even they will generally need a lifting system at some point.

Most wells, however, need a lifting system to effectively remove the gas. The most common method is rod pumping, which uses a surface pump run by a cable and a rod that moves up and down to pump the gas out of the well. The most common pump is called a "horse head" pump because the

Fig. 2-4. *A Beam Pumping Unit with Horse Head*

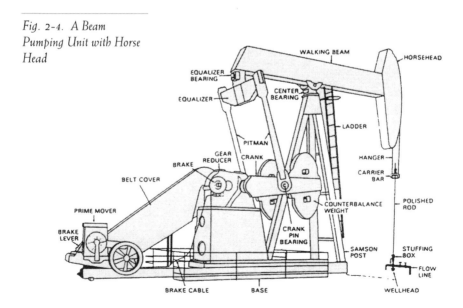

end that feeds cable into the well is shaped like a horse head (Fig. 2-4). The pumps use weights to help the motor lift the rod in the pumping mechanism. Other lifting devices may lie under the surface of the earth. These units sit closer to the gas deposit and pump the gas to the surface.

Wells rarely pump constantly. It takes time for the gas to seep through the rock layer beneath the well. For efficiency, producers set the pumps to run only part of the time to allow the gas time to accumulate in the well.

Natural gas production volumes in the U.S. vary somewhat from year to year, but have been relatively steady, staying between 510 and 545 billion cubic meters annually in the 1990s. Canada adds another 100 to 150 billion cubic meters annually and Mexico contributes a bit less than 30 billion cubic meters to the North American gas production total, which tends to be a bit over 700 billion cubic meters annually (Table 2-2).

Table 2-2. Natural Gas Production, 1995

In billion cubic meters	
U.S.	535
Canada	148
Mexico	28
Total North America	711
Total World	2,130

Processing

The gas processing industry gathers, conditions, and refines natural gas into useable forms for a variety of applications. Raw natural gas is primarily methane, but also contains many other hydrocarbon gases, including ethane, propane, butane, pentane, hexane, and heptane (Fig. 2-5).

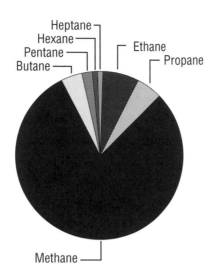

Fig. 2-5. Raw Natural Gas by Component

An average breakdown of raw natural gas by component. A variety of other hydrocarbon gases may be present in the methane mixture. These are generally removed and sold separately.

Hydrocarbon	Amount, %	Nonhydrocarbon	Amount, %
Methane	70-98	Nitrogen	trace-15
Ethane	1-10	Carbon dioxide	trace-1
Propane	trace-5	Hydrogen sulfide	trace occasionally
Butane	trace-2	Helium	trace-5
Pentane	trace-1		
Hexane	trace-0.5		
Heptane	none-trace		

The gas processing industry handles more than 18 trillion cubic feet of natural gas annually in the U.S., the equivalent of about 3 billion barrels of oil. The gas is refined into useable natural gas, liquefied petroleum gases, motor fuel components, and raw materials for petrochemicals.

Natural gas is found in three basic forms—associated gas, non-associated gas, and gas condensate. Associated gas is found in oil reservoirs, either dissolved in the oil or separate but mixed with the oil deposits. It is extracted from the wells with the oil. It separates at the head of the well. In the early days of the natural gas industry, all gas was associated gas found while drilling for oil.

Non-associated gas is found in reservoirs separate from oil. These wells are drilled specifically for the natural gas beneath the surface. This gas is often called "gas-well gas" or "dry gas". Today, approximately 75% of all U.S. natural gas production is non-associated gas.

Many oil wells produce neither liquids nor gases, but something in between. It is not a gas because its density is too high and it is not a liquid. These are called gas condensate reservoirs and they are usually deeper wells with higher pressures.

Natural gas has a widely varying composition, but the principal constituents are methane and ethane. Most gas also has heavier components such as propane, butane, pentane, and heavier hydrocarbons that are removed during processing. Each component has a distinct weight, boiling point, and other physical characteristics. This makes it possible to separate the components. Natural gas that has a high content of heavy components is considered rich or wet. Lean or dry gas has relatively low levels of the heavy gases.

Natural gas may also contain water, hydrogen sulfide, carbon dioxide, nitrogen, helium, and other components that may either dilute or contaminate the gas. All natural gas is processed to remove unwanted elements that would interfere with pipeline transportation or marketing. Natural gas in pipelines is almost entirely methane and ethane with very low amounts of moisture or contaminants. Pipelines generally have their own specifications for the quality of gas needed for transportation.

In processing natural gas, producers find there are several hydrocarbon liquids that are separated and sold as separate products. These include:

- Ethane exists as a liquid only under very high pressures or at very low temperatures. It is used as a feedstock for ethylene, the most important basic petrochemical produced today
- Propane is used as a feedstock for production of ethylene and propylene, and as a gas for heating fuel, engine fuel, and industrial fuel

- Iso-butane is an important ingredient in high-octane gasoline. It is also used in production of methyl tertiary butyl ether (MTBE), which is an ingredient of reformulated motor gasoline
- Natural gasoline is a mixture of pentanes and heavy hydrocarbons, with small percentages of butane and iso-butane. It is used as a motor fuel component

Carbon dioxide is removed and injected into oil wells to enhance recovery. Hydrogen sulfide is both poisonous and corrosive, so it is removed and processed into elemental sulfur.

Gas processing starts at the well when gas is separated from crude oil. Gas and other components are removed from the oil at the wellhead to stabilize it for pipeline transport. The gas is gathered, treated, compressed, and piped to a facility for final processing to produce quality natural gas and marketable gas liquids. Final processing in the plant involves extraction of the natural gas liquids from the gas stream and fractionation (separation) of

Table 2-3.
Gas Processing Profile

State	# Plants	Gas processed (mmcfd)	NGL	NGL % mB/D
Texas	237	11,502	725	40.9
Louisiana	68	12,734	272	15.3
Oklahoma	79	2,748	174	9.8
Wyoming	39	3,030	103	5.8
New Mexico	28	2,122	163	9.2
Kansas	16	2,803	97	5.5
Other U.S.	156	13,416	241	13.5
Total U.S.	623	48,355	1,775	100.0

Source: *Oil & Gas Journal*

the gas liquids into components. More processing is usually required to treat and condition both the natural gas and the liquids.

There are two basic ways that components in the gas are separated—absorption or fractionation. *Absorption* removes components from the gas through contact with an absorbing oil. Separating components by controlling the temperature is called *fractionation*. This process takes advantage of the difference in boiling points among separate products. Natural gas liquids are generally fractionated by boiling the lighter products to separate them from the heavier products.

There are more than 600 gas processing plants in the U.S. They are primarily found in six states, which account for more than 70% of the country's total gas processing capacity and almost 90% of the natural gas liquids production. The six big gas processing states are Texas, Louisiana, Oklahoma, Wyoming, Kansas, and New Mexico (Table 2-3). Average gas plant capacity is 110 million cubic feet/day. Plants range from less than 1 million cubic feet/day to more than 2 billion cubic feet/day. There are also about 70 fractionating plants in the U.S.

The gas processing industry in the U.S. consists of about 250 companies, with the 20 largest gas processing companies producing about 35% of total U.S natural gas and about 75% of total natural gas liquids. The U.S. produces about 648 million barrels of natural gas liquids annually, about 1.8 million barrels a day. U.S. supply also includes refinery production and imports.

Transportation and Storage

3

lthough natural gas can be moved in other ways, pipelines are by far the dominant mode of transport in this industry.

There are three groups of pipelines: gathering, trunk or transmission, and distribution. Gathering lines connect individual wells to field gas-treating and processing facilities or to branches of a larger gathering system. Most gas wells flow naturally with sufficient pressure to supply the energy needed to force the gas through the gathering line to the processing plant. In low-pressure gas wells, small compressors may be located near the well to boost the pressure in the flowline to a level sufficient to move the gas to the processing plant. In some cases, several well flowlines feed into a larger line, which then carries the combined flow to the plant.

Flowline lengths vary, but they are generally only a few miles long. The lines are relatively small with diameters ranging from two to four inches. Operating pressures also vary, but they generally operate at several hundred psi, and sometimes up to 2,000 psi. The length, operating pressure, size, and throughput of gas well flowlines depend on the capacity of the well, the type of gas produced, process plant operating conditions and location, and other factors.

From the field processing facilities, gas enters the transmission pipeline system for movement to cities where it will be distributed to individual businesses, factories, and residences. Distribution to final users is handled by utilities that take custody of the gas from the gas transmission pipeline and distribute it through small, metered pipelines to individual customers.

Gas transmission systems can cover large geographical areas and can be hundreds of miles long. Transmission lines operate at relatively high pressures. Compressors at the beginning of the line provide the energy to move the gas through the pipeline. Then compressor stations sited along the line are used to maintain the required pressure. The distance between compressors depends on the volume of gas, the line size, and other factors. Capacity can be increased by adding compressors.

Transmission pipelines are made of steel pipe buried below the surface of the ground. Individual sections of pipe are joined by welding, and the pipe is externally coated to protect against corrosion. Pipe size ranges up to 60 inches in diameter.

Operation of a gas transmission system that moves gas over a large geographic area with several compressor stations and other facilities is a complex control challenge. Computers and sophisticated communications systems allow pipeline operators to better deliver the required volumes of gas while minimizing malfunctions in the system.

The U.S. gas transmission system has more than 300,000 miles of piping, not including local distribution lines. These pipes must be monitored around the clock to keep accurate data on flow, content, and condition. Most companies use supervisory control and data acquisition systems (SCADA) to maintain data from remote sites, including unmanned stations. Major investments were made in the pipeline system in the 1980s and early 1990s, improving the system's capacity to areas in the Northeast, West Coast and Florida. However, the pipeline industry is still making improvements in capacity, efficiency, and cost effectiveness, since transportation costs still make up a large portion of the consumer's price for natural gas (Table 3-1).

Table 3–1
Gas Pipeline Construction
in 1998.

Region	4-10 in.	12-20 in.	22-30 in.	32+ in.	Total Miles
U.S.	1,405	287	835	577	3,104
Canada	398	85	190	50	723
Latin America	50	118	120	151	439
Asia-Pacific	328	2,219	731	306	3,584
Europe	1,028	459	97	2,195	3,779
Middle East	--	57	--	--	57
Africa	--	40	27	621	688
World Total	3,209	3,265	2,000	3,900	12,374

Projects already started or set to begin in 1998, with completion expected in 1998.

Region	4-10 in.	12-20 in.	22-30 in.	32+ in.	Total Miles
U.S.	64	117	645	2,650	3,476
Canada	360	498	1,420	2,814	5,092
Latin America	--	846	794	4,251	5,891
Asia-Pacific	841	3,120	1,726	1,252	6,939
Europe	58	589	1,874	3,240	5,761
Middle East	522	19	166	829	1,536
Africa	--	--	--	449	449
World Total	1,845	5,189	6,625	15,485	29,144

Projects starting in 1998, to be completed in 1999 or later.
Source: Oil & Gas Journal

Capacity

Capacity requirements—for any given pipeline or the entire industry—can vary. Demand for natural gas has generally been increasing by 2% or 3% annually but there are no guarantees that demand will increase on a particular line. Demand is estimated and projections are made of future needs, and a compromise is struck between building a pipeline large enough to handle any possible volume requirements and one that is capable of handling only the current demand.

If too much excess capacity exists for long periods of time after pipeline construction, the profitability of the system suffers. If a smaller line is built and volume requirements exceed its capacity, the system must be expanded. Systems can be expanded by either adding more pumping or compression horsepower, or by installing an additional pipeline along all or a portion of the route. Installing parallel pipeline is called looping.

Most pipelines are designed with some excess capacity, or are designed so capacity can be increased by adding compression or pumping horsepower. The increase in throughput that can be obtained by adding horsepower is limited by the maximum allowable operating pressure of the system. Maximum operating pressure is determined by codes and regulations applicable to the pipe size, weight, and steel composition and by the area in which the line is located.

Pipeline design

Key elements of pipeline design include several items:

- *Pipe diameter*. The larger the inside diameter of the pipeline, the more fluid can be moved through it, assuming other variables are fixed
- *Pipe length*. The greater the length of a segment of pipeline, the greater the total pressure drop
- *Specific gravity and density*. The density of the gas is its weight per unit volume

- *Compressibility.* At high pressures and temperatures, the compressibility factor of gas will deviate. Design calculations must account for compressibility at base conditions and at high pressure or temperature conditions
- *Temperature.* Temperature affects pipeline capacity both directly and indirectly. In gas pipelines, the lower the operating temperature, the greater the capacity, assuming fixed variables
- *Viscosity.* Viscosity is the property of a fluid that resists flow and it is an important element when calculating pipe size and pump horsepower requirements
- *Friction factor.* Friction factors vary according to the roughness of the inside pipe wall

There are several formulas that can be used to calculate the flow of gas in a pipeline. These account for the effects of pressure, temperature, pipe diameter and length, specific gravity, pipe roughness, and other elements. The main difference in each formula is the size range in which it tends to be most applicable and the treatment of pipe friction.

Prime movers

A prime mover is an engine, motor, or turbine that supplies the horsepower needed by a pump or compressor to move the gas through the pipeline. Prime movers are generally selected for horsepower output and efficiency. The availability of energy to power the prime mover and the cost of that energy must also be considered. The initial cost of the unit is compared with that of other units; maintenance costs must be factored in as well. Prime movers include electric motors, gas turbines and diesel and internal combustion engines. Electric motors and gas turbines are the most popular.

There is no average compressor or pump station size, nor an average pump or compressor size within a station. A small gas-gathering system compressor station may have only one 100 hp compressor unit; a large main line transmission station may have several units totaling 30,000 hp or more. A typical system includes compressors driven by prime movers with horsepower outputs totaling several hundred thousand horsepower.

To calculate the amount of horsepower required to drive a compressor, the theoretical horsepower needed to increase the gas pressure from suction pressure to discharge pressure must be determined, allowing for losses in the compressor. Because gas is a compressible fluid, more terms must be used in the calculation.

Electric motors are popular for sites with electric lines installed because the initial cost is often lower than that of other prime movers. Electric motors are also easily adapted to automatic control and remote operations. Maintenance requirements are generally low. Electric motors can pose a hazard in explosive environments, so they are often placed in motor enclosures. Other considerations in selecting an electric motor as a prime mover include insulation, physical specifications of the motor and mounting arrangement, and the need for air filter equipment. Abrasive, high-moisture, chemically corrosive or other severe environments may require special precautions or considerations.

Gas turbine prime movers are widely used to drive pipeline pumps and centrifugal compressors in natural gas service. A variety of turbines is available. Generally, the industrial turbine is a moderate speed machine, operating at 6,000 to 8,000 rpm. Aero-derivative turbines, which operate at higher speeds, may also be used. Liquid fuel or natural gas can be used to provide energy to the gas-producer section of the turbine. The atomized fuel or gas is mixed with compressed air and ignited in this section. The resulting hot exhaust gases turn the turbine shaft. Gas turbines have a higher initial cost than electric motors and can cost more to maintain. Ambient temperatures also have a significant effect on turbine capacity and must be considered. They often offer a significant amount of fuel flexibility, able to run on natural gas, diesel and other gaseous fuels as needed.

Control and scheduling

Pipeline control systems regulate pressure and flow, start-and-stop pumps or compressors at stations along the line, and monitor the status of pumps, compressors, and valves. In a large pipeline system, many of the supervisory functions are performed from a central location.

One of the pipeline operator's most important functions is scheduling the volumes of each product transported by the pipeline to ensure delivery to the customer at the desired time. He/she also must account accurately for all volumes shipped. This is a simple task, when product changes are infrequent and the number of shippers and customers is small. A complex system, with many customers and a variety of products, requires frequent changes in flow and operating conditions. Scheduling and accounting become quite complex.

Pigs

Pipeline "pigs" and spheres are used to clean pipelines and to separate different fluids in a pipeline. Pigs can also be used to monitor conditions and problems that could lead to failure. Pigs generally have a steel body with rubber or plastic cups attached to seal against the inside of the pipeline and to allow pressure to move the pig along the pipeline. Different types of brushes and scrapers can be attached to the body of the pig for cleaning and other functions.

Pipeline pigging is done for several reasons:

- To remove wax, dirt, and water from the pipeline
- To separate products to reduce the amount of interface between different types of products
- To control liquids in a pipeline when testing, drying or purging
- To inspect pipelines for defects such as dents, buckles, or corrosion
- To apply internal coating to the walls of the pipeline for corrosion protection

Measuring

Natural gas can be measured with meters—orifice, positive displacement, turbine, and other types of meters. These devices measure the volume of gas flowing in the line. In recent years, emphasis on the heat content of the gas has resulted in techniques for monitoring the Btu content of the flowing gas steam. In addition to traditional methods that use periodic sampling or chromatography, acoustic measurement of gas Btu content is also possible.

Base conditions, such as atmospheric pressure and temperature must be determined before flow can be measured. Base conditions are spelled out in gas contracts. Meters also need other data such as flowing temperature and pressure, gas specific gravity, and the compressibility of the gas at the flow conditions.

Gas can be measured either by volume or mass. Mass flow measurement has been popular in recent years. It measures gas flow in pounds per hour, whereas volume flow measures gas flow in cubic feet per hour. The two are related by the specific gravity of the flowing fluid. For some fluids, particularly natural gas liquids whose physical behavior is not very predictable, mass measurement is more accurate than volume measurement.

When pipeline systems are interconnected, gas from several sources is mixed in one pipeline. This has brought about the need to measure the heating value of natural gas, in addition to its volume or mass. Accurate measurement of heating value permits customers to be charged fairly and the producer to receive a fair price.

The common unit of heating value is the *Btu*—the amount of heat required to raise the temperature of a given mass of water 1°F at a specified temperature. Heating value is often further defined as either gross heating value or net heating value. Gross heating value of natural gas is the number of Btu evolved by the complete combustion at constant pressure of one standard cubic foot of gas with air. The temperature of the gas, air, and products of combustion is at 60°F. All water formed by the combustion reaction is condensed to a liquid state. For net heating value, the gross heating value is determined and then the latent heat of vaporization of water formed by the combustion reaction is subtracted.

Storage

Storage facilities are an important element in pipeline transportation systems. Storage allows flexibility in pipeline operations and minimizes unwanted fluctuations in pipeline throughput and product delivery. Natural gas storage is needed to meet peak demands that may be much higher than the pipeline's average throughput. It would not be possible to vary production from gas wells feeding into the transmission line as widely and as frequently as demand varies. Natural gas demand is highly dependent on weather, for instance, and a method to handle these fluctuations is required.

Natural gas is generally stored underground as a gas or as liquefied natural gas in aboveground or belowground tanks. As a gas, it can be stored underground in rock or sand reservoirs that have suitable permeability and porosity. The gas is injected under pressure, and then pressure in the reservoir is used to force the gas out when it is needed. When demand is high, gas is withdrawn from the reservoir and combined with gas being delivered by the transmission pipeline. Natural gas can also be stored in depleted oil or gas fields. Salt caverns and aquifers are also used for underground storage of natural gas. When demand is low, gas is diverted from the transmission pipeline into storage. Some of the gas in the reservoir must be used as cushion gas to allow withdrawal and injection of usable gas. Storage reservoirs are ideally located near consuming centers and near the transmission pipeline and its compression facilities.

Natural gas stored as a liquid (LNG storage) is a way to do so compactly. When liquefied at about minus 260°F, its volume is reduced to 1/600th of the gaseous volume. LNG storage is required at baseload plants—complete plants that include purification, liquefaction, storage, and regasification—as well as at terminal plants, where LNG is received from tankers and regasified as needed, and at peak-shaving plants, where natural gas is stored as liquid to meet peak demands.

Underground and aboveground tanks and frozen earth storage are all used to store LNG. Because it must be stored at very low temperatures to maintain a liquid state, insulation is one of the most important elements of LNG storage design. In frozen earth storage, a cavity is excavated in the ground. Pipes are then installed around the cavity to circulate refrigerant, freezing the earth and forming an impermeable barrier. The cavity is topped with an insulated cover to contain the LNG. Aboveground LNG storage tanks are double walled with insulation between the inner and outer walls. Aboveground storage is used in the majority of LNG peak-shaving and base load plants.

Underground concrete storage tanks are also used for LNG storage. They are considered applicable for large storage quantities. These tanks must also be heavily insulated. From storage, LNG is pumped to a vaporizer that regasifies the natural gas for delivery to customers.

Trading

4

deregulation of the natural gas industry and pricing set by supply and demand, has opened the industry to traders. As in any commodity market, traders try to buy low and sell high to turn a profit; gas is bought and sold as a commodity.

Pipelines providing basic transportation of gas from one location to another connect regions of supply to market areas. Some pipelines bridge the gap between other pipelines or storage areas. Finally, the gas reaches end users. It is here, at the burner-tip or burning point, that the flow of gas stops and it is consumed.

There are several types of end users—some of which are regulated, depending on what type of business they are in. For example, local distribution companies (LDC) provide a pipeline or distribution system and gas supply for consumers in towns and cities. Since LDCs are considered public utilities, they are subject to rate approval and regulation by their state Public Utility Commission (PUC). Other end users include non-regulated industrial consumers that burn gas to generate heat, powering machines that manufacture their products. Cogeneration plants use natural gas to produce heat, creating steam that in turn generates electricity. Commercial end users burn gas to provide space heat and heat for hot water, as well as power for air conditioning units. These consumers include offices, schools, hotels, and restaurants.

Electric utilities are the single largest end users of natural gas in terms of the volume of natural gas consumed per user. They burn large quantities of natural gas to generate electricity, which they then sell to electricity buyers. Because they are utilities, the price they can charge for electricity is regulated by their state PUC.

This is in the process of changing as the electricity industry undergoes deregulation, and the price of electricity will also be set by supply and demand. Electricity is already traded as a commodity on a limited basis, and some states are well on the way to deregulating their industry. This means that if natural gas prices rise to the point that it is no longer economical to make the energy conversion to electricity—based on the price received for the electricity—the utility will switch to alternate fuels or generate more power from facilities that burn other fuels such as coal or nuclear energy.

Although they are neither producers nor end users, marketing companies play a big role in the business activity on a pipeline. Also called resellers or third parties, they are in the business of capturing profits from opportunities presented. Their best-known function here is as trading companies—buying and reselling natural gas for a profit. These companies are not paid a fee by anyone, but earn the difference (or take a loss) between the price they pay for gas and the price at which they sell it. As a result of deregulation, any company is free to buy and sell natural gas to anyone. In addition, it is entitled to contract for pipeline capacity on almost any pipeline system. The ability to enter the market with opportunities like these has led to the explosive growth in the number of natural gas trading companies. The traders are working to make a spread—the difference between the buy price and sell price. In addition, many producers, LDCs, and electric utilities have established marketing or trading departments within their respective organizations to participate in these potentially profitable opportunities or to specialize in administering the services necessary to conduct business with natural gas.

Each day trading companies look for areas of excess supply or high demand. If they find a region that is temporarily oversupplied, e.g., they can inexpensively buy and take title to the supply when they sell and transfer title to another party, they capture a profitable spread in between. Transactions like this can occur either at the same place or where the gas is consumed. The goal is the spread.

Service, marketing, and trading companies are important to the natural gas industry for several reasons. As service providers, they perform necessary administrative business procedures, at a low cost, for companies that don't have established departments or the know-how to perform them. As traders, they keep supply and demand in balance by searching for profitable arbitrage opportunities where there are discrepancies.

Supply

As we have seen, North America has an abundant supply of this particular natural resource. Much of our natural gas comes from a few regions and must be transported for use. Some is less expensive to produce because it is found in shallower depths, and some is more expensive because it is more difficult to drill.

But the biggest factor affecting supply in North America is price. The higher natural gas prices are, the more incentive producers have to look for more supplies. As prices fall, wells that are only marginally profitable will be closed to ensure that maintenance and production costs do not exceed sales revenue. Also, the risk of loss in new drilling projects increases relative to the potential reward when evaluating prospective wells.

Natural disasters can temporarily affect supply. Due to the vast amount of production in offshore wells in the Gulf of Mexico, hurricanes pose a threat to the stability of this supply region. Whenever a hurricane threatens, producers evacuate workers and stop production. This causes a temporary shortage. If a storm actually damages these rigs, as Hurricane Andrew did in 1992, shortages become more serious. During Andrew, several rigs were damaged and made inoperable, and supply couldn't be restored for about six months. Natural gas prices soared as buyers scrambled to replace lost supply. During the outage, supply from throughout the U.S. and Canada was re-routed to make up for the lost supply from the Gulf of Mexico area. Prices around the country continued to rise as demand outweighed supply. However, when production from the damaged rigs resumed, supply caught up with demand and natural gas prices gradually fell back to pre-disaster levels.

On a smaller scale, wellheads can freeze during prolonged periods of intense cold weather. When this happens, the wells in a specific production area become inoperable and the supply from that region is temporarily unavailable to the market. As temperatures return to normal, production is restored, and the gas is again available to the market.

Demand

The demand side of the natural gas market is more dynamic than one might expect. Natural gas has more uses than just heating and air conditioning. Although natural gas is primarily used as a fuel to generate heat, there are also more obscure uses. Crude oil producers in California will sometimes use natural gas to extract more crude oil from old, low-pressure wells. This is accomplished by injecting highly pressurized natural gas into the ground beneath the oil reserves to increase the crude oil reserve pressure. This type of use accounts for only a tiny fraction of overall demand, however.

Industrial companies represent the largest portion of natural gas demand, powering machines and heavy equipment. Residential consumption also accounts for a large portion of total natural gas demand. Residential consumption is very straightforward—home heating, or as a fuel for stoves, fireplaces, and hot water heating tanks.

Power generation is the third largest market for natural gas. Electric utilities and independent power producers use natural gas to power gas-fired turbines to generate electricity.

The level of demand for natural gas rises and falls as a result of changes in price and for several other reasons as well. By far the most important force altering the level of demand is weather. Cold weather strongly affects demand for residential and commercial heating. Also, hot weather affects gas demand, as electric utilities use more gas to generate more electricity for air conditioning.

The economy also effects demand. A strong economy that generates demand for steel products, for example, will cause steel manufacturers to run their equipment at maximum capacity to manufacture additional products. Their demand for natural gas increases as they use it to heat ovens over additional work shifts. Demand for gas, in terms of consumption, is less sensitive to changes in price than the supply is. This is true as prices increase, but even more apparent when prices decrease. That is due to the nature of the uses for natural gas, more consumers do not eagerly rush into the market to buy if prices fall. However, if prices fall to a certain level, it is not uncommon for producers to shut-in wells in a matter of a few hours.

Transportation

A pipeline nomination is a notification given by a third party shipper to a pipeline. It requests the pipeline recognize, account for, and physically implement a transportation transaction for that shipper. If the shipper is planning to transport gas on a particular pipeline from point A to point B, it must notify that pipeline of its intentions through a nomination. A nomination must include all details needed to ensure that the pipeline can perform the requested service properly. Nominations generally include:

1. Shipper's transportation contract number
2. Delivering party's transportation contract number
3. Start date
4. Stop date
5. Shipper's receipt location
6. Shipper's receipt amount

7. Shipper's delivered location

8. Shipper's delivered amount

9. Receiving party's transportation contract number

Because natural gas transactions are done on a daily basis, natural gas pipelines monitor their systems on a day-to-day basis as well. With little variation, physical operators of wellheads, gathering systems, and the pipelines themselves begin measuring and accounting for volumes flowing through their respective systems at 7 A.M. central time and end at 7 A.M. the following day. The typical nomination deadline is 10 A.M. central time for gas to flow the following day. As a result of these deadlines, trading activity is busiest in the early morning hours as traders conduct their business for the following day.

Once it receives a nomination from a shipper, the pipeline follows a confirmation procedure, matching all the details of the shipping party to those of the delivering party, and the details of the delivering party to the details of the receiving party. If any of the relevant information does not match, the nomination will not be confirmed and must be resubmitted.

Once a nomination is confirmed, the pipeline schedules the gas to flow. It notifies its operations personnel to expect the amount of the gas in the shipper's nomination to flow through the shipper's designated receipt meter and the shipper's designated delivery meter on the start date and every day thereafter until further notice. There is typically more gas flowing through meters other than the amount in one shipper's nomination, so pipeline operators designate the amount specified in the shipper's nomination at a particular meter as "gas supply intended for the shipper's account". The pipeline will usually furnish a report to all the parties in the transaction when the scheduling process has been completed successfully.

Scheduling constitutes only what the pipeline expects to happen. Because measurements are made over a 24-hour period, pipeline operators do not know how much gas was actually received and delivered until the day after it is scheduled to flow. For this reason, the pipeline must allocate the amount of gas that actually flowed through a meter (or meters) among the various shippers who nominated gas at that point for the day.

Allocations are typically done by first granting the full amount scheduled by those shippers using firm transportation contracts, and then prorating the remaining amount among shippers with interruptible contracts. Allocation is done at all meters on a pipeline's system. This means that pipelines are continuously measuring and accounting for the amount of gas scheduled to flow and for the amount that actually flowed through the pipelines. That is, the pipeline is constantly juggling *scheduled* amounts versus *allocated* amounts, always lagging by one full day.

Pipelines must also balance scheduled and allocated receipts into its system with scheduled and allocated deliveries out of its system. Most pipelines allow for a 3% "scheduled imbalance tolerance" for any given day if the pipeline can physically handle the impact, or if the shipper has an existing imbalance that it wishes to work off by overreceiving or overdelivering until the imbalance is eliminated.

Two basic types of transportation contracts were referenced above: firm and interruptible; firm transportation has priority over interruptible. It cannot be disrupted by the pipeline for any reason other than natural disasters. Interruptible transportation has low priority in terms of reliability because it can be disrupted by the pipeline for any reason. Under either type of contract, shippers pay what is known as a commodity rate, expressed in $/MMBtu. This rate varies according to the time of year and the distance of transportation. There may also be in-kind fuel charges, where delivered volume is less than received volume by a percentage. Firm contracts also carry a reservation charge.

Physical transactions

Natural gas is bought and sold under different types of contracts. Each contract, however, references the following standard specifications:

1. buyer
2. seller
3. price
4. amount (amount per day)
5. receipt/delivery point (title transfer point)
6. tenure (number of days)
7. terms and conditions

Special "terms and conditions" typically outline details such as payment dates, quality specifications, and specifics regarding performance, along with other items. There are three types of performance obligations that differentiate contracts—interruptible or swing contracts, baseload contracts, and firm contracts.

Under an interruptible contract, the buyer and seller agree on a specific price and amount in the transaction, but limit the term of the transaction. Both parties agree that neither party is obligated to deliver or receive the exact volume agreed to. These are referred to in the industry as swing deals—day-to-day contracts in which both price and volume can swing up and down.

Baseload agreements are similar to interruptible agreements in that each party agrees that neither party is obligated to deliver or receive the volume in the transaction. However, there is a general understanding that each party will, on a best-effort basis, deliver and take the volume in the transaction.

Firm contracts, however, have legal recourse embedded in them for instances where either party fails to take or deliver the agreed-upon volume at the agreed-upon price for the tenure of the contract. These contracts are only used in transactions where the supply and demand for the gas is expected to be 100% reliable.

Financial markets

The monetary value of natural gas is reflected in terms of its price. The price of gas, like any other freely traded commodity or security, fluctuates when the perceived value of that product changes. The difference in opinion between buyers and sellers over what the perceived value of a commodity should be is what constitutes a market. The price, or market value, is a reflection of what the majority of the market perceives to be the value of the product, and is what the commodity is actually worth at that specific time (Figs. 4-1 and 4-2).

Fig. 4-1. Natural Gas Prices, 2nd Quarter 1998

Fig. 4-1. Electricity Prices, 2nd Quarter 1998

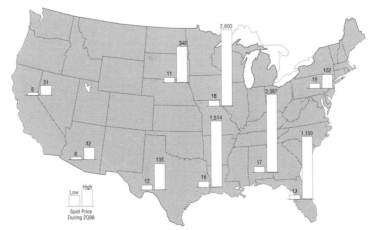

The supply and demand balance of any commodity is constantly moving in or out of equilibrium as a result of changes in opinion. By continuously searching for discrepancies between supply and demand, or discrepancies between market participant's perceived values of natural gas, traders are invariably pushing the market into equilibrium. As a result, trading companies help maintain an orderly market.

The standard pricing formula for natural gas is in dollars and cents per MMBtu to flow on a daily basis.

In the day-to-day market for physical natural gas, buyers and sellers conduct the majority of their transactions with each other over the telephone. Electronic bulletin boards are available for physical trades to be cleared at a few major trading points by third-party operators. Natural gas traders maintain lists of contacts at other companies whom they know to be traders of gas on a particular pipeline, at a specific point, or in a designated region of the country. It is through these contacts that most transactions are done and market information is disseminated.

Although the daily market for natural gas is active, the majority of gas trading occurs during the last week of each month. This period of time is known in the industry as bid-week. It is the time when market participants buy and sell the majority of their gas requirements and available volumes of gas for the following month. Gas transactions are prepared in terms of volume per day, but the standard industry practice is to deal for a month at a time. During bid-week, trading volume is heaviest as producers try to sell their core supply, end users try to buy for their core needs, and marketing companies try to get in between the two.

Electricity is also traded as a commodity on a limited basis, but the volume of trading is increasing. As deregulation progresses, it should one day mirror natural gas trading. Commodity status is one of the many similarities between the natural gas and the electric industries, and these similarities are pulling the industries together. Similar knowledge and skills are helpful in trading both electricity and natural gas. In fact, many of the pioneers in the electric trading market were the gas traders!

Natural Gas Basics

5

n atural gas is a clean, economical, widely-available fuel used in more than 58 million homes and in more than 60% of the manufacturing plants in the U.S.

Almost one-quarter of the gas consumed in the U.S. is produced domestically from wells in the central part of the country. Gas is transported from these wells by pipelines throughout the country becoming more expensive the further it must be shipped. Even when shipped a great distance, natural gas is generally less expensive than oil products, although it is more expensive than coal on the basis of heating values.

Combustion of natural gas in the U.S. produced 318 million metric tons of carbon emissions in 1996 (the latest official government figures available at this writing). The industrial sector was responsible for the largest share of those emissions (about 45%) followed by residential, commercial, and electricity generation. If no additional carbon reduction measures are enacted, carbon emissions from natural gas combustion are expected to escalate by another 100 million metric tons by 2010. Natural gas consumption is expected to increase more rapidly than consumption of any other major fuel through 2010. Its use is expected to increase in all sectors, but consumption for electricity generators is expected to more than double by 2010, taking advantage of high efficiencies of combined-cycle units and the low capital costs of combustion turbines. By 2010, the generating capability of combined-cycle plants may increase by more than sixfold from the 1998 capacity, as generating capacity of combustion turbines more than doubles.

One factor contributing to the popularity of natural gas is its domestic availability. Unlike oil—largely imported from other countries and often from somewhat politically unstable parts of the globe—most of the U.S. natural gas we consume comes out of the ground in the middle of our nation. Disputes in the Middle East cannot create shortages here.

Even as natural gas consumption booms into the next decade or two, domestic supplies will provide for the country's needs. More than 80% of any increase would likely come from domestic reserves, with the remainder coming from increased imports, primarily from Canada.

Two-thirds of any production increase would come from onshore resources in the lower 48 states with the remainder coming from Alaska and offshore resources. Roughly 75% of current proved reserves are located onshore in the lower 48 states. Continued technology improvements make development of the onshore conventional resources more economical. Wellhead prices are expected to increase only moderately through 2010, reflecting increased consumption and its impact on resources.

Chemical advantage

Another advantage natural gas possesses is its chemical composition. Natural gas is basically methane, which has one carbon atom and four hydrogen atoms.

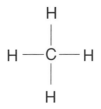

Table 5-1. Carbon Emissions from Fossil Fuel Generation Technologies

Technology	Heat Rate Btu/kWh	Carbon #/MMBtu	Emissions #/MWh
Coal-Fired Technologies			
Existing Capacity	10,000	57	571
New Capacity	9,087	57	519
Advanced Coal Technology	7,308	57	418
Natural Gas-Fired Technologies			
Conventional Turbine	10,600	32	336
Advanced Turbine	8,000	32	253
Existing Gas Steam	10,300	32	326
Conventional Combined-cycle	7,000	32	222
Advanced Combined-cycle	6,350	32	201
Fuel Cell	5,361	32	170

Because of methane's chemical structure, burning natural gas creates fewer carbon emissions than the other fossil fuels. Natural gas allows fuel users to use the same number of Btus while emitting less carbon (Table 5-1).

Natural gas is composed of hydrocarbon molecules that range from one to four carbon atoms in length. Gas with one carbon atom in the molecule is methane (CH_4), two is ethane (C_2H_6), three is propane (C_3H_8), and four is butane (C_4H_{10}). All are paraffin-type hydrocarbon molecules. The percentages each in the gas vary from field to field, but methane is by far the most common hydrocarbon (Table 5-2). Many natural gas fields produce almost pure methane. It's the gas burned in homes. When propane and butane burn, they give off more heat than methane, and they are often distilled from natural gas and sold separately. Liquefied petroleum gas (LPG) is made from propane gas.

Inerts are nonhydrocarbon impurities in natural gas that don't burn. A common inert is carbon dioxide, a colorless and odorless gas. Because it

Table 5-2 *Average Midcontinent Natural Gas Hydrocarbon Composition*

Methane (CH$_4$)	88%
Ethane (C$_2$H$_6$)	5%
Propane (C$_3$H$_8$)	2%
Butane (C$_4$H$_{10}$)	1%

doesn't burn, the more carbon dioxide natural gas contains, the less valuable the gas. In some reservoirs, carbon dioxide is the majority gas. Large fields of almost pure carbon dioxide, thought to have been formed by the chemical reaction of volcanic heat on limestone, occur in New Mexico, Utah, and Colorado. Carbon dioxide can be used for inert gas injection (an enhanced oil recovery process) in depleted fields. Nitrogen, another inert, is also a colorless and odorless gas used for inert gas injection.

Helium (He) is a light gas used in electronic manufacturing and filling dirigibles. The Hugoton-Panhandle gas field—the largest natural gas field in North America—gives the U.S. a virtual monopoly on world helium production. Gas from the Hugoton-Panhandle field contains 0.5 to 2% helium that is separated from the natural gas as it is produced. Helium is not common in other natural gas fields.

Hydrogen sulfide (H$_2$S) is a gas that occurs either mixed with natural gas or by itself. It is not an inert, and it is very poisonous gas—lethal in very low concentrations. The gas smells like rotten eggs and can be detected in extremely small amounts. It is associated with the salt domes of the Gulf of Mexico and ancient limestone reefs of Mexico, West Texas, and Louisiana. Hydrogen sulfide is common in Alberta, Canada, parts of Wyoming, California and Utah, and in the Middle East. Hydrogen sulfide is extremely corrosive, and when it is mixed with natural gas, it causes corrosion of the metal tubing, fittings, and valves in a well. Hydrogen sulfide must be removed before natural gas can be delivered to a pipeline. Sweet natural gas has no detectable hydrogen sulfide, whereas sour natural gas has detectable amounts of it.

Solution gas

Because of high pressure in the subsurface reservoir, a considerable volume of natural gas occurs dissolved in crude oil. The solution of gas/oil is expressed as a ratio—the cubic feet of natural gas dissolved in one barrel of oil in that reservoir under subsurface conditions. (Volume measurements are made under surface conditions.) Generally, as the pressure of the reservoir increases with depth, the amount of natural gas that can be dissolved in crude oil increases. When the oil is lifted up a well to the surface, the pressure is dropped and the gas, called solution gas, bubbles out of the oil.

The producing gas-oil ratio (GOR) of a well is the number of cubic feet of gas the well produces per barrel of oil. (The volume measurements are made under surface conditions.) Usually, a gas well has a GOR greater than 150,000. Oil wells have GORs less than 15,000.

Nonassociated natural gas is not in contact with oil in the subsurface trap. A nonassociated gas well produces almost pure methane. Associated natural gas occurs in contact with crude oil in the subsurface. Associated gas occurs both as gas in the free gas cap above the oil and gas dissolved in the crude oil. It contains other hydrocarbons besides methane.

Condensate

In high-pressure and high-temperature conditions underground, some hydrocarbons are found as a gas until they are pumped out of the well and the temperature falls; then the liquid hydrocarbons condense out of the gas. This liquid, called condensate, is mostly gasoline. Condensate is also called casing-head gasoline, drip gasoline, or natural gasoline. It doesn't have the high octane of gasoline that is produced in refineries, but refiners will pay almost as much for it as for crude oil, and mix it with high-octane gasoline in refineries. Natural gas that contains condensate is called wet gas, and natural gas without condensate is called dry gas. When condensate, along with butane, propane, and ethane, can be removed from natural gas, it is then called natural gas liquid.

Measurement

The English unit of volume measurement for natural gas is 1,000 cubic feet (cf) (Table 5-3). Because gas expands and contracts with pressure and

Table 5-3 Natural Gas Measurements and Conversions

Volumetric Unit	Heating Unit
1 therm	100,000 Btu
1 dekatherm	1,000,000 Btu
1,000 cubic feet	1,000,000 Btu
1 quad	1 quadrillion Btu
1 kilojoule	948 Btu
1 cubic foot	1,026 Btu
1 cubic meter	35.3 cf
1 tonne LNG	48.7 Mcf
1 barrel of crude petroleum	5.8 million Btu
1 pound bituminous coal	12,000 Btu
Oil/Coal Volume	**Natural Gas Volume Equivalent**
1 barrel of crude oil	5,650 cubic feet
1 ton of bituminous coal	23,400 cubic feet

Cubic foot (cf) is the prevailing volumetric unit used in the U.S., the United Kingdom, and by the gas industry in Canada; sometimes specified as a standard cubic foot (scf). It is the amount of gas that would fill a volume of 1 cubic foot at 60°F and at the atmospheric pressure at sea level, 14.7 psi.

Cubic meter (cm) is the most frequently used volumetric measure elsewhere, except when measuring liquefied natural gas, which is generally measured in metric tonnes. Governments in Canada use the kilojoule (kj) heating-value unit, but the more widely accepted heating-value unit is the British thermal unit (Btu).

temperature changes, measurement is made at or is converted to standard conditions—usually 60°F and 14.7 psi—also called standard cubic feet (scf). The abbreviation for 1,000 cubic feet is Mcf (a million cubic feet is MMcf). A billion cubic feet is Bcf and a trillion cubic feet is Tcf. Condensate is measured in barrels per million cubic feet of gas, abbreviated BCPMM.

As mentioned earlier, the unit used to measure heat content of fuel in the English system is the British thermal unit (Btu—approximately equivalent to the heat given off by burning one wooden match. Pipeline natural gas ranges from 900 to 1,200 Btus per cubic foot. Heat content varies with hydrocarbon composition and the amount of inerts in the gas. Natural gas is sold to a pipeline by volume in thousands of cubic feet, by the amount of heat when burned in Btus, or a combination of both. There can be a Btu adjustment clause in a pipeline contract. Gas bought at a certain price per Mcf is then adjusted for the Btu content. As a rule, one cubic foot of natural gas has about 1,000 Btus of heat.

In the metric system, the volume of gas is measured in cubic meters (m^3). A cubic meter is equivalent to 35.315 cf. Heat is measured in kilojoules. A kilojoule is approximately equal to 1 Btu. The Btus in an average barrel of crude oil are equivalent to the Btus in 6,040 cf of average natural gas, called barrels of oil equivalent (BOE).

Usage and trends

Between 1950 and the late 1980s, electricity generators were third among the major users of natural gas, after industrial and residential users. In the late 1980s, they began to slip into fourth position, following commercial users, and they remain there today. Oil and coal prices fell in the 1980s while gas prices were fairly constant, thus oil and coal took a larger share of the growing electricity generation market while gas use remained flat. Gas consumption continued to grow in the commercial sector, eventually surpassing electricity sector consumption.

U.S. consumption of natural gas has been growing between 1 and 2% annually through the late 1990s (Table 5-4). Consumption dipped to 16,221 tcf in 1986 and set a record high of 22,101 tcf in 1972. The industrial sector has officially accounted for a great portion of the growth in consumption, but a major reason industrial use is booming is that gas used in nonutility electricity generation is considered industrial consumption. Between 1986 and 1997, commercial demand for gas jumped almost 40%—much of this increase coming from nonutility electricity generation.

Official utility demand for natural gas has been volatile (Table 5-5). This is the sector where natural gas has the most intense competition from other fuels. Utility demand reached a recent high of 3.197 tcf in 1995, then fell to 2.732 tcf in 1996. Demand jumped again in 1997 and 1998. A sharp increase in gas prices was the major reason for the drop in utility demand in 1996. Prices were even higher in 1997, but strong economic growth and reduced output at nuclear plants boosted utility demand for gas.

Table 5-4
U.S. Natural Gas Supply
and Demand, Bcf

	1995	1996	1997	1998
Production				
Texas	6,330	6,449	6,432	6,480
Louisiana	5,108	5,241	5,475	5,650
Other states	8,068	8,061	7,939	7,940
Total Production	**19,506**	**19,751**	**19,846**	**20,070**
Imports				
Canada	2,816	2,883	2,896	2,934
Mexico	7	14	16	16
LNG	18	40	78	80
Total Imports	**2,841**	**2,937**	**2,990**	**3,030**
Supplemental gas	110	109	116	120
Losses	-1,137	-679	-919	-900
Supply from storage	415	2	27	0
Exports	154	153	157	155
Total Consumption	**21,581**	**21,967**	**21,903**	**22,165**

*Table 5-5. U.S. Energy
Consumption Trends,
Trillion Btu*

Year	Energy Cons.	Oil Cons.	Natural Gas Cons.	Total Petroleum	Oil/Gas % Total Energy
1960	44,569	20,067	12,699	32,766	73.5
1965	53,343	23,242	16,097	39,339	73.7
1970	67,143	29,537	22,029	51,566	76.8
1975	70,546	32,731	19,948	52,679	74.7
1980	75,955	34,202	20,394	54,596	71.9
1985	73,981	30,922	17,834	48,756	65.9
1990	81,283	33,553	19,296	52,849	65.0
1995	87,205	34,663	22,163	56,826	65.2
1998*	91,810	36,760	22,760	59,520	64.8
*estimates					

Gas demand is expected to continue increasing in the utility and industrial sectors due to competitive pricing and continuing economic growth. A warm winter in any year can hurt gas demand figures for that year as it slows industrial sector growth and drives down demand in the residential sector.

In recent years, domestic gas production has risen in response to increases in both demand and average wellhead price. Domestic output hit a peak of 22.65 tcf in 1972 and slipped to a recent low of 16.9 tcf in 1986. Since then, output has increased at an average rate of 1.5% annually. Consumption over the same period has increased by 2.9% annually.

Additional imports have been providing a large share of the increase in consumption. Imports of natural gas, mainly from Canada, have been increasing. Mexico also contributes a small amount to our gas supply. However, the great majority of the U.S. natural gas demand is supplied by domestic production.

In the future, supply provided to electric generators is expected to become more important to the gas industry. The U.S. Energy Information Administration projects that electricity generators will become the second largest consumers of natural gas, behind the industrial sector, by 2010. Consumption of natural gas for electricity generation is projected to reach 12.2 Tcf in 2010—more than four times the 1996 level (Figs. 5-1, 5-2).

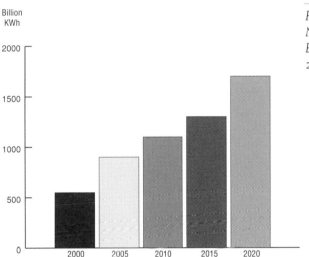

Fig. 5-1. Projected Natural Gas-Fired Electricity Generation, 2000-2020

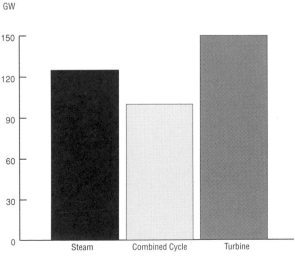

Fig. 5-2. Projected Natural Gas-Fired Electricity Generation Capacity, 2010

Electricity generators can be expected to take a greater interest in natural gas pipeline capacity expansion by investing in some projects or by making long-term contracts. Merging gas and electricity companies could occur when the advantage of arbitraging the two markets becomes apparent. Electricity generators might also increase their direct ownership of natural gas resources or make long-term contracts with producers in efforts to reduce price volatility.

Electric Power History

6

lthough man has experimented with electricity for many hundreds of years, the history of the electric power industry is little more than 100 years old. The early days of electricity were dominated by inventive minds and entrepreneurs. One invention led to another and another, and soon the individuals charting the path to an electrified nation became figureheads for massive companies with names that are still highly visible, especially Westinghouse and Edison.

In 1800, Alessandro Volta invented the electric battery. Known as a Voltaic battery, it provided the first continuous source of electricity that scientists of the era used in their experiments. In 1808, Englishman Humphrey Davy produced an arc of light by sending a battery-powered electric current through the space between two carbon rods. In 1831, Michael Faraday invented the dynamo, which would produce an electric current when turned by a steam engine.

Such early discoveries with this new energy form helped inventors create machines that had never before been imagined, machines that led to the industrial revolution and automated industrial processes, and to the lighting of America.

The electrification of the U.S. began with Thomas A. Edison's invention of the electric light bulb in 1878 (Fig. 6-1). That same year he founded the Edison Electric Light Company to generate, transmit, and distribute electric power. In 1882, Edison started the nation's first investor-owned electric utility with Pearl Street Station—a direct current (dc) system capable of powering 7,200 incandescent lamps within a one square mile area.

Fig. 6-1.
Thomas A. Edison

Fig. 6-2.
George Westinghouse

MAJOR LEGISLATION AFFECTING THE ELECTRIC POWER INDUSTRY

This list is by no means all-inclusive. It offers only a quick rundown of major legislation that created and maintained the regulatory environment utilities have lived in for most of their existence. It is the unraveling of this web of legislation that is creating today's competitive environment.

The Tennessee Valley Authority Act of 1933. Under this law the federal government provided electric power to states, counties, municipalities, and nonprofit cooperatives. It was the steady continuation of federal responsibility to adopt navigation, flood control, strategic materials for national defense, electric power, relief of unemployment, and improvement of living conditions in rural areas. The Tennessee Valley Authority (TVA) was also authorized to generate, transmit, and sell electric power.

The Public Utility Holding Company Act of 1935 (PUHCA). PUHCA was enacted to break up the large and powerful trusts that controlled the nation's

Following Edison's success in New York, other entrepreneurs started their own systems. George Westinghouse (Fig. 6-2), using the discovery of Nikola Tesla, developed an alternating current (ac) system that permitted electricity transmission over much greater distances than Edison's dc system. Direct current flows only in one direction. Alternating current reverses flow direction at regular periods. It consists of a succession of cycles, and the number of cycles per second is the current's frequency. The majority of today's electricity is alternating current, although batteries are direct current.

Westinghouse formed Westinghouse Electric Company in 1886 and began selling ac electrical systems, in direct competition with Edison's dc systems. Edison stood by his dc technology, claiming that ac electricity is much more dangerous than dc. (Both are dangerous!)

ac vs dc

The ac technology, however, had a great asset in its transmitability. Dc could only be transmitted for about a mile, while ac allowed Westinghouse to locate central generating stations at the source of fuel and transmit the power over greater distances.

The development of the ac system was not a total solution for power delivery, however. The two types of systems could not be linked together, and the electric systems sometimes served different types of customers with different types of motors. Most systems needed two sets of transmission wires to accommodate both ac and dc.

Westinghouse provided a solution by developing a system by which electricity was produced by a polyphase ac generator at a central station. Polyphase generators generally have three phases, giving them the advantage of completely smooth power transfer. The alternator in a car produces dc power, but is actually a 3θ ac power plant with a diode rectifier to deliver the dc power a car battery needs. In Westinghouse's new system, electricity was sent to a substation that, like an alternator, would regulate and deliver the type of power a customer needed. This system became known as the Niagara Central Station Plan.

In 1883, Westinghouse won the contract to light the Chicago Columbian Exposition, the World's Fair that showcased incandescent electric lighting for the public. It was the first large-scale demonstration of alternating current.

Even by 1900, however, electricity had made few inroads into the growing cities of the U.S. Less than one in 15 city households had electric current and those that did generally only had capability to run lights. Only 3% of factories used equipment run by electric motors. Electric appliances would not gain popularity until the 1920s, although electric washing machines and stoves were available by 1910 thanks to pioneers such as

electric and gas distribution networks. PUHCA gave the Securities and Exchange Commission the authority to break up the trusts and to regulate the reorganized industry to prevent their return. PUHCA was recently overhauled since many argued that PUHCA's regulations were impediments to the development of an efficient electricity market.

The Federal Power Act of 1935 (Title II of PUHCA). This act was passed at the same time as PUHCA. It was passed to provide for a federal mechanism, as required by the Commerce Clause of the Constitution, for interstate electricity regulation. Prior to this time, electricity generation, transmission, and distribution was almost always a series of intrastate transactions.

Rural Electrification Act of 1936. This act established the Rural Electrification Administration (REA) to provide loans and assistance to organizations providing electricity to rural areas and towns with populations under 2,500.

(continued)

MAJOR LEGISLATION AFFECTING THE ELECTRIC POWER INDUSTRY (CONT.)

REA cooperatives are generally associations or corporations formed under state law. The predecessor to this act was the Emergency Relief Appropriations Act of 1935, which performed the same function.

Bonneville Project Act of 1937.
This act created the Bonneville Power Administration (BPA), which pioneered the federal power marketing administrations. The BPA was accountable for the transmission and marketing of power produced at federal dams in the northwest. In 1953, the BPA first guaranteed the bonds of and a market for small energy facilities built and financed by public utility districts.

Flood Control Act of 1944.
This act formed the basis for the later creation of the Southeastern Power Administration in 1950 to sell power produced by the U.S. Army Corps of Engineers in the Southeast; and the Alaska Power

Frederick Maytag and George Hughes of Hotpoint.

Still, electricity was a high technology commodity that drew a great deal of attention from both the media of the day and of the public. Thomas Edison—dubbed "the Wizard of Menlo Park"—started it all with his three-wire electric incandescent lighting system. He enjoyed a great deal of celebrity in his day.

National electrification

The cost of electrifying urban America was covered primarily by big business. Electrification was quite expensive. Investors needed to build electric plants, construct miles upon miles of transmission and distribution lines, and hire a large work force to run the system. Each house had to be wired to use electricity before its residents could become customers.

Samuel Insull, an Edison protege who worked for the Chicago Edison Co., found that electric companies suffered from high fixed costs associated with generating plants and transmission equipment. However, operating costs— expenses associated with fuel—were quite low. He found that more revenue could be generated by adding customers on each system. He slashed electricity prices and aggressively marketed the benefits of electric power in an attempt to increase customers. Many electric companies of the time gave away light bulbs and electric irons to lure customers to their systems. They were searching for profits through what's known as economies of scale.

Insull found another benefit from an economy of scale: the more time a generating plant was in use, the greater the efficiency factor. Efficiency yielded higher profits and lowered costs per kilowatt-hour (kWh) for customers. Also, utilities used separate generating plants to meet various customer loads, such as the daytime industrial load and the evening residential load or the morning and afternoon streetcar load. Insull pioneered the concept of the base load generating plant, one facility to meet all basic electric needs on the system, with others held in reserve for peak load conditions.

Insull also promoted the concept of state regulation of small utilities in order to establish franchise territories and set prices. This idea also caught on. By 1916, 33 of the 48 states had public utility commissions to grant utilities exclusive rights to operate in certain areas in return for agreements to serve all existing and future customers at set prices. Regulated utilities, so-called "natural monopolies", have been the primary service providers ever since, although the regulations directing the industry have changed over time. (See sidebar concerning legislation affecting the industry.)

PUHCA

Electricity became immensely popular, with great public demand for electrification. As

Administration in 1967 to both operate and market power from two hydroelectric plants in Alaska. Although the Southwestern Power Administration's authority after World War II came from the Flood Control Act of 1944, it was established using the executive branch's emergency war powers authority to satisfy the growing demands from weapons development and domestic needs.

Energy Supply and Environmental Coordination Act of 1974 (ESECA). This act allowed the federal government to prohibit electric utilities from burning natural gas or petroleum products.

DOE Organization Act of 1977. In addition to forming the Department of Energy, this act provided authority for the establishment of the Western Area Power Administration (WAPA) and transferred power-marketing responsibilities and transmission assets previously managed by the Bureau of Reclamation to WAPA. WAPA's authority was extended through the Hoover Power Plant Act of 1984. This act also

(continued)

MAJOR LEGISLATION AFFECTING THE ELECTRIC POWER INDUSTRY (CONT.)

transferred the other four power marketing administrations from the Department of the Interior to the Department of Energy.

The Public Utility Regulatory Policy Act of 1978 (PURPA). PURPA was passed in response to the unstable energy climate of the late 1970s. PURPA sought to promote conservation of electric energy. Additionally, PURPA created a new class of nonutility generators, small power producers, from which, along with qualified cogenerators, utilities are required to buy power.

The Energy Tax Act of 1978 (ETA). This act, like PURPA, was passed in response to the unstable energy climate of the 1970s. The ETA encouraged conversion of boilers to coal and investment in cogeneration equipment and solar and wind technologies by allowing a tax credit on top of the investment tax credit. It was later expanded to include other renewable technologies. However, the

the nation's appetite grew, the utilities began consolidating into major conglomerates. By 1930, only a handful of electric utilities remained. In response, Congress enacted the Public Utilities Holding Company Act (PUHCA) in 1935 to break the conglomerates into smaller pieces confined to specific geographical areas.

Four types of electric utilities emerged:

- *Investor-owned electric utilities* financed by private investors, selling to both retail and wholesale customers
- *Municipally owned electric utilities* owned by the municipality in which they operate
- *Federally owned electric utilities* generating power at federally owned hydroelectric projects
- *Member-owned rural electric cooperatives* providing electric power to members

For the next few decades, electricity prices fell as utilities built larger, more efficient generating facilities, high-voltage transmission lines to connect the plants, and distribution lines to serve the ever-expanding customer base. Then came the Arab oil embargo in 1973, which triggered a terrible recession. This event coincided with the large power plants' economy of scale reaching their limits and brought the cycle of decreasing costs and lower rates to a screeching halt. Between 1974 and 1981, the average residential price for electricity more than doubled. This brought a change in attitude among customers. Consumer groups and large industrial users challenged rate increases. Environmentalists mounted opposition to new plants and transmission lines.

The March 1979 accident at Pennsylvania's Three-Mile Island Nuclear Plant fueled fears of nuclear power and halted construction of new nuclear plants, a technology once hailed as able to one day render electricity so inexpensive that there would be no need to measure usage for billing purposes.

PURPA

To avoid the need for new power plants, a way was sought to decrease peak demand on the electric system. The Public Utility Regulatory Policy Act of 1978 (PURPA) was conceived and imposed by the federal government to champion energy conservation and encourage industrial users to generate their own electricity. It also advocated the development of renewable energy sources, such as hydro, solar, and wind power.

PURPA obligated electric utilities to buy the extra power generated by industrial customers and from renewable energy sources. As a result, a whole new class of generating firms—non-utility generators—was born, reopening the door of competition in the electric industry.

incentives were curtailed as a result of tax reform legislation in the mid 1980s.

National Energy Conservation Policy Act of 1978. This act required utilities to provide residential consumers free conservation services to encourage slower growth of electricity demand.

Powerplant and Industrial Fuel Use Act of 1978. This act succeeded the Energy Supply and Environmental Coordination Act of 1974, and extended federal prohibition powers.

The Clean Air Act Amendments of 1990 (CAAA). These amendments established a new emissions-reduction program. The goal of the legislation was to reduce annual sulfur dioxide emissions by 10 million tons and annual nitrogen oxide emissions by 2 million tons from 1980 levels for all manmade sources. Generators of electricity are responsible for large portions of the sulfur dioxide and nitrogen oxide reduction. The program instituted under the CAAA

(continued)

MAJOR LEGISLATION AFFECTING THE ELECTRIC POWER INDUSTRY(CONT.)

employs a market-based approach to sulfur dioxide emission reductions, while relying on more traditional methods for nitrogen oxide reductions.

The Energy Policy Act of 1992 (EPACT).
This law created a new category of electricity producer, the exempt wholesale generator, which circumvented PUHCA's impediments to the development of nonutility electricity generation. The law also allowed the Federal Energy Regulatory Commission to open up the national electricity transmission system to wholesale suppliers.

Unfortunately, PURPA imposed artificially high prices on utilities when buying alternative power. e.g., Southern California Edison Company had to pay 15 cents/kWh for solar power, despite the fact that electricity costs at the time were only two or three cents on the wholesale market. Decreasing fuel costs, plus the development of smaller, more efficient natural gas generators, made it possible for independent power producers (IPP) to finance new plants and generate electricity far more economically than the established utilities.

The Wholesale Market

The wholesale market for electricity was opened in 1992, triggering fierce competition for a share of the $43 billion market (the market now exceeds $50 billion). FERC estimates that completely open access could save customers $3.8 billion to $5.4 billion annually. Although customers may benefit, utilities worry that they may be left with liabilities from the existing electric power system infrastructure. New competitors don't have to include infrastructure investments in the pricing, so they may be able to underprice the utilities.

These costs—called "stranded costs"—are a major topic of debate in the process of deregulation that is currently under way. Infrastructure that made perfect sense under the rules and regulations mandated by the government at the time they were purchased are now uneconomical in a free market. The big question is who should pay for these "assets" and how should they be valued.

Industry statistics

Today's $200 billion U.S. electric power industry is considered the largest industry in the country. There are more than 3,000 electric utilities, most of which are public utilities. The U.S. has almost 2,000 public utilities, and they generate 14% of the country's electric power. There are almost 900 cooperative utilities, generating 8% of the country's power. Investor-owned utilities (IOUs) number close to 200 and generate 76% of the electricity. Six federal utilities generate the remaining 2%. There are many more public utilities, but they are smaller than the IOUs, which generate by far the greatest amount of electricity.

Coal is traditionally the most popular fuel for electric generating plants, although in the past few years, that has changed. Natural gas is the fuel of the 90s (and beyond), at least in the U.S. Natural gas has gained popularity because of its reasonable cost and clean burning properties.

Coal-fired generation still represents more than 40% of the U.S. capacity, with more than 300,000 MW installed. Natural gas-fired electricity generating facilities have climbed to 20%, with about 150,000 MW up and running. Almost all the new capacity now being planned or constructed is fired on natural gas. Traditional gas companies are expanding into electric power, as they recognize the potential of investing in both big energy commodities—natural gas and electricity. Both are traded as commodities, and holding both allows a company to maximize its profits from the Btus. Natural gas generating plants have overtaken all other technologies in popularity (see chapter 5–Natural Gas Basics).

Nuclear power provides almost 100,000 MW of the country's electricity, about 14%, but nuclear power's share will slide in the future. No more plants are being built and some of the older ones are beginning to be retired. Petroleum fuels a little less than 10% of our nation's power plants.

Hydroelectricity accounts for more than 20,000 MW of U.S. generating capacity, about 3%. Other renewable energy sources, such as wind and solar power, now account for more than 10% of our capacity with about 80,000 MW installed. Renewable energy is very clean but also more expensive than the fossil fuels that generate the majority of our power. As technology advances, the cost of installing these types of plants is rapidly becoming more competitive.

This is an exciting moment in the timeline of the electric power industry. Deregulation will no doubt affect all aspects of the industry, from the popularity of the various fuels and technology, to the marketing and public relations of utilities. The basic pieces of the electricity industry may not change very much, but their relationships and ownership will probably be greatly affected. The number of utilities operating in the country is expected to shrink—some say dramatically. But our society is extremely reliant on electricity for everything from coffee in the morning to electricity to run our computers at work. So regardless of the changes the industry must endure, the business of power generation will continue, and the basic components will remain.

Electricity has nearly come full circle, from an open field populated by entrepreneurs and unregulated businesses to a fully monopolized, government-regulated industry, to a commodity on the brink of deregulation that will once again open the field to entrepreneurs and unregulated businesses. The utilities of today are working to prepare for the open market and the unregulated subsidiaries are already participating in the portions that are already open. As the circle is completed, natural gas will be the fuel that propels the industry forward into the converged Btu industry that is waiting around the corner.

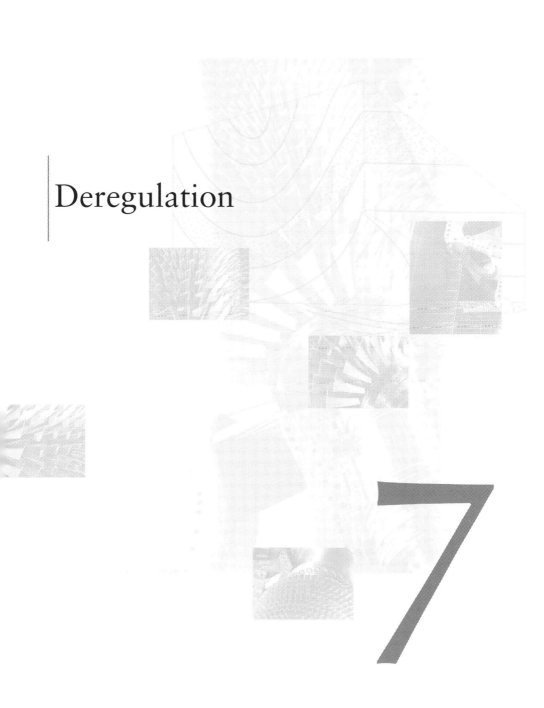

Deregulation

7

t he electric power industry in the U.S. is composed of traditional electric utilities—including power marketers—and nonutility power producers. Traditional electric utilities are composed of investor-owned, publicly owned, cooperative, and federal utilities. They are generally vertically integrated companies, providing generation, transmission, distribution, and/or energy services for all customers in a designated service territory. There are about 3,200 electric utilities in the U.S., although that number is in a constant state of flux due to an unprecedented string of mergers and acquisitions brought about by industry restructuring.

Traditional utilities are going through a serious rethinking of business objectives in light of this restructuring. Investor-owned utilities (IOUs) must decide whether they want to remain aligned with the generation side of the business or focus on the transmission and distribution functions of the electricity chain. Publicly owned utilities are struggling with how they will compete in an open market against the heavyweight IOUs that previously did not pose a competitive threat because of protected service territories. Federal power administrations are debating critical ownership issues. As federal entities, there is question whether they should even be competing against private enterprise. Rural cooperatives are working to identify and retain their niche in the electricity marketplace.

Some publicly owned utilities are quite large. Three federal agencies, the Tennessee Valley Authority, the Bonneville Power Administration, and the Western Area Power Administration (WAPA) together own or market more than 40% of total U.S. hydroelectric capacity. Bonneville and WAPA, plus the Southeastern and Southwestern Power Administrations, market power generated by the U.S. Army Corps of Engineers and the Bureau of Reclamation of the Department of the Interior. Due to their long-depreciated assets and low operating costs, their federal hydroelectric plants have very low costs for generation. Privatization of these federally owned power companies is under consideration.

The majority of the state and municipal utilities and cooperatives only distribute power to their communities. Most are too small to generate electricity and purchase it in the wholesale market. Purchased power accounts for approximately 70% of total costs for most of the municipal utilities. They have preferred access to the cheap federal hydroelectric power, whereas IOUs receive access only if municipal utilities do not need it.

Publicly owned electric companies also have access to cut rate financing. The municipalities that own them can issue tax-exempt bonds for approved improvements.

There is a gap between publicly and privately owned utilities. The public companies sell their power 16% to 20% cheaper on average than IOUs. There is considerable controversy regarding whether this gap is fully explained by the public companies' access to inexpensive hydro resources and tax exempt financing or whether the gap shows a real difference in efficiencies. These issues must be addressed as deregulation proceeds.

Power marketers who buy and sell electricity generally do not own or operate generation, transmission, or distribution facilities. Still, they are often considered "electric utilities". As of July 1998, 557 individual entities had received approval of their rate tariffs from the FERC to sell wholesale electric power. This number includes 337 independent power marketers, 91 affiliated power marketers, 32 affiliated power producers, 73 investor-owned utilities with market-based rates, and 24 other utilities with market-based rates.

The volume of wholesale electricity sold in recent years has skyrocketed. While natural gas volumes sold by the top 10 marketers rose by 17.7% between 1996 and 1997, power sales by the same 10 companies jumped 340% during the same period. Nearly as much wholesale power was sold in the first quarter of 1998 as in all of 1997.

The almost 2,000 nonutility generators are also re-examining their position in the deregulating landscape. Many of these facilities were established under PURPA, which required conventional utilities to purchase nonutility power at the utility's "avoided generation cost" (what it would cost a generator to produce the electricity). In some cases, this was a fairly high figure, providing an attractive opportunity for savvy investors. In today's electricity market, with wholesale electricity available at 2-3 cents/kWh, the electricity from many nonutilities would be uncompetitive if sold on the open market. Recognizing this, utilities are buying out existing contracts with the nonutilities, confident they will be able to recoup the buyout cost through reduced generation costs into the future.

Pricing and Growth

Retail electricity prices are projected to decline by 1% annually through 2020 because of greater competition and declines in electricity production costs. Production costs have fallen 1.8% annually since 1982 and are expected to continue falling but at a slower rate. The decline in production cost is the result of higher plant efficiencies, demand growth, fuel cost declines, and staff reductions. In 1982, coal-fired plants used 250 employees per GW; by 1995, that number fell to 200. Similarly, gas-fired plants reduced staff from 138 per GW in 1982 to less than 100 per GW in 1995.

Residential electric rates are expected to fall 19% by 2020, commercial rates 21%, and industrial rates 24%. These projected drops assume full competition in the electricity industry, in contrast to trends apparent in today's markets, where industrial customers appear to be getting larger rate reductions than residential and commercial customers.

As generators and cogenerators attempt to adjust to the evolving structure of the electricity market, they are also faced with slower growth in demand. Historically, demand has been related to economic growth. This positive relationship will continue, but the magnitude of the ratio is uncertain.

During the 1960s, electricity demand grew by more than 7% a year—nearly twice the rate of economic growth. In the 1970s and 1980s, however, the ratio of electricity demand growth to economic growth declined to 1.5 and 1.0, respectively. Several factors contributed to this trend, including increased market saturation of electric appliances, improvements in equipment efficiency, utility investments in demand-side management programs, and legislation establishing more stringent equipment efficiency standards. For similar reasons, a continued decline is expected.

Natural gas prices paid by electricity suppliers are expected to rise by 0.7% annually, from $2.70 per thousand cubic feet in 1996 to $3.22 in 2020. Gas-fired electricity generation has been estimated to increase by 376%, from 462 to 1,583 billion kWh. Offsetting these increases are declining coal prices, declining capital expenditures, and improved efficiencies for new plants. Oil prices paid by utilities are expected to increase by 29%. As a result, oil-fired generation is expected to decline by more than 56% by 2020.

Changing consumer markets could mitigate the slowing of electricity demand growth seen in these projections. New electric appliances are introduced frequently. No one foresaw the growth in home computers, facsimile machines, copiers, and security systems—all powered by electricity. If new uses of electricity are more substantial than currently expected, they could partially offset future efficiency gains.

With the number of U.S. households projected to rise by 1.0% a year through 2020, residential demand for electricity grows by 1.5% annually. Although many regions currently have surplus base load capacity, strong growth in the residential sector will result in a need for more peaking capacity. Between 1996 and 2020, generating capacity from gas turbines and internal combustion engines is expected to more than triple.

Electricity demand in the commercial and industrial sectors is expected to grow by 1.2 and 1.3% a year, respectively, through 2020. Annual commercial floorspace growth of 0.8% and industrial output growth of 1.9% drive this increase.

In addition to sectoral sales, cogenerators in 1996 produced 149 billion kWh for their own use in industrial and commercial processes, such as petroleum refining and paper manufacturing. By 2020, these producers are expected to maintain about the same share of total generation, increasing their own-use generation to 165 billion kWh as demand for manufactured products increases.

Restructuring

The electric power industry in the U.S., which until recently has been operated as a regulated monopoly, is now being restructured to operate in a competitive market. The changing environment is the result of actions taken by large consumers and regulations from federal and state governments. In shedding its traditionally monopolistic status, the industry is following in many ways changes enacted in the natural gas, airline, trucking, and long-distance phone companies. The electric utility industry in the U.S. will emerge as a more competitive business (Figs. 7-1 and 7-2).

As the electric power industry splits into unbundled service groups, significant consolidation is taking place within several of them. Generation will be most exposed to competition. New players are also entering the industry.

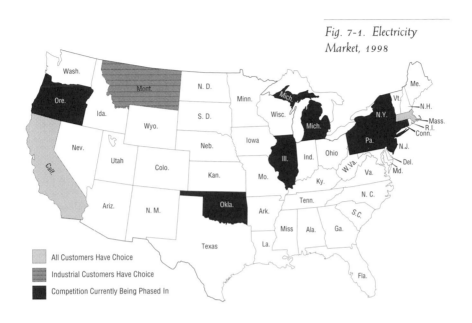

Fig. 7-1. Electricity Market, 1998

All Customers Have Choice

Industrial Customers Have Choice

Competition Currently Being Phased In

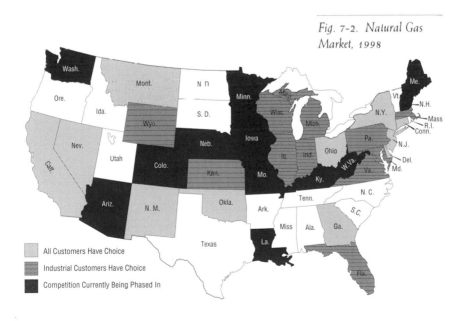

Fig. 7-2. Natural Gas Market, 1998

All Customers Have Choice

Industrial Customers Have Choice

Competition Currently Being Phased In

Marketing, trading, and risk management will assume greater roles in the evolving electricity industry, requiring insights and experience of trading companies and advertising agencies.

Significant convergence is evident across business sectors as well. The natural gas and electricity industries are melding together, capitalizing on their similar structures, markets, and business characteristics. The telecommunications industry is also being drawn into the electricity industry, as savvy marketers explore novel ways to package electric and communication products and services. Tracking developments in the electricity industry now involves much more than surveying the previous year's major news in generation, transmission, and distribution.

The electricity business in the process of transition to a competitive market is the largest remaining regulated industry in the U.S. Its traditional, vertically integrated structure will in all probability be segmented at least functionally into its three component parts—generation, transmission, and distribution. The proposals and issues that will govern such a transition are being addressed in federal and state legislation and debated in state regulatory hearings.

Regulation of the electric power industry is complex, in large part because of the division of regulatory and legislative powers between the states and the federal government. As in other markets, interstate commerce falls under federal rules and intrastate business is under state domain. Each state has a state regulatory commission overseeing all regulated industries. Several federal bodies address interstate trade. FERC is the main federal agency for the power industry.

The distinction drawn between state and federal turf is complicated in electricity because power exchanges happen constantly, beyond any single entity's control, in integrated AC electricity networks. Oversight of these transactions, including the price of power generated for sale on the grid, the price of transmission services, and regulation of transmission access, is FERC's responsibility. This is true, even if they occur on lines which begin and end in the same state, as long as they connect to the overall grid. In practice, FERC regulated about 65% of the nationwide transmission network because it has jurisdiction over only the investor-owned portion. Its authority over the remainder is limited.

FERC has traditionally regulated power sale and transmission prices in interstate transactions through a cost-plus formula using the historic cost of the transmission or generating asset. Prices are calculated to offer a "fair" rate of return. These prices remain in place until the utility applies for and receives approval for a rate increase (or a decrease, theoretically).

Regulatory turf distinctions are further complicated by the industry's distinction between transmission and distribution. Distribution assets fall under state jurisdiction, but in many instances, it is difficult to fully distinguish whether a power line is a transmission or distribution line. In general, high-voltage lines traversing great distances are transmission lines, whereas lower voltage lines running for short distances to deliver power to end users are distribution lines. However, two lines of the same voltage could have different uses. The lines between federal and state turf are blurred here. With few exceptions, however, FERC has jurisdiction over transactions involving the transmission grid.

The transmission market has more than 150 energy control centers that are responsible for the stable operation of the power systems and transmission grids in their areas. The control centers maintain schedules for generation and exchange power among other control areas over their interconnections. At the next level are 20 cooperative power pools—formal agreements among utilities to coordinate some or all of their activities to improve economic performance. Power pools typically coordinate maintenance schedules among member utilities, carry out central dispatch of generating units, and help with joint capacity planning.

There are also 10 regional reliability councils covering North America. They are members of the North American Electric Reliability Council (NERC), a nonprofit organization promoting reliability of electricity supply (Fig. 7-3).

Fig. 7-3. NERC Regions of the U.S. and Canada

The NERC regions include:

- East Central Area Reliability Coordination Agreement (ECAR)
- Electricity Reliability Council of Texas (ERCOT)
- Mid-Atlantic Area Council (MAAC)
- Mid-America Interconnected Network (MAIN)
- Mid-Continent Area Power Pool (MAPP)
- Northeast Power Coordinating Council (NPCC)
- Southeastern Electric Reliability Council (SERC)
- Southwest Power Pool (SPP)
- Western Systems Coordinating Council (WSCC)
- Affiliate member Alaska Systems Coordinating Council(ASCC)

Hearings and, in some cases, legislation, are driving the current process for change at the federal and state levels. Industrial consumers want to choose the electricity supplier that meets their needs economically, reliably, and efficiently. Utility consumers who see differences in prices in neighboring states—especially in states with higher-than-average electricity rates, like California and in the Northeast—are promoting competition to try and make lower rates available. In fact, California, New York, and most of the New England states opened at least part of their retail electric power markets to competition in 1998.

Independent power producers expect expansion and increased profitability from an unconstrained market. Regulators are experimenting with alternative forms of regulation because some groups believe that the traditional practice of regulating a utility's rate of return does not contain incentives sufficient to encourage efficient utility operations. Utilities are dissatisfied with legislation that has given a competitive advantage to nonutility electricity producers and limits holding company activities.

Change began with FERC Orders 888 and 889, issued in 1996 to encourage wholesale competition. Order 888 addresses the issues of open access to the transmission network and stranded costs. Order 889 requires utilities to establish electronic systems to share information about available transmission capacity. Subsequently, many states are actively pursuing or investigating deregulation and retail competition legislation in one form or another. Legislative proposals on electric power restructuring have been introduced into the U.S. House of Representatives and the Senate, although, as of mid 1998, none had received congressional approval or been signed into law.

Issues such as recovery of stranded costs, divestiture of assets, increased mergers, renewable energy incentives, energy efficiency investments, reliability, and the timing of retail competition are critical, due to the degree of importance electricity holds in this country's economic and social well-being.

With competition on the horizon, IOUs are reducing staff and reorganizing their companies to reduce costs. IOUs have taken advantage of lower fuel prices by modifying their fuel acquisition procedures. They're buying out older, more expensive fuel contracts and purchasing less expensive coal in the spot market. An increase in power purchases over the past decade has hindered efforts to lower costs for some utilities. On the other hand, nonfuel operation and maintenance costs have remained stable, indicating that some progress in cost reduction has been achieved, but also indicating that more may be needed.

Some of the largest IOUs are expanding their business investments in energy service companies; oil and gas exploration, development, and production; foreign ventures; and, more recently, telecommunications ventures. Mergers, acquisitions, and divestitures are also gaining momentum in the electric power industry.

Changing ownership of generating assets is increasingly commonplace in the electricity industry. Deals are being announced with surprising frequency in an industry that has, historically, fiercely protected its assets. The divestiture push is being driven by the desire to make electricity markets more competitive, which requires the elimination—or at least reduction—of market domination by a few large companies. Some industry experts have predicted more than $100 billion in power plant transactions in the next two or three years.

The trend does not spell an end to electric utility involvement in power generation, of course. Some of the most active bidders in recent auctions are other electric utilities. The industry is separating into those companies that want to reduce involvement in generation and those companies that want to augment it, and which have the financial resources to do so. Buyers must weigh their purchasing decisions against the current cost of new combined-cycle generation, which averages $500-600/kW.

Some experts predict that the country is moving toward a structure in which electric power generation is concentrated in about 50 large companies. Under that same scenario, transmission could come to be dominated by about 10 large regional companies with three to five generation firms in each transmission region. Also, divestiture and asset sales help determine an asset's market value, which can then be used in establishing stranded cost levels.

Stranded costs

Stranded costs are of major concern to many industry groups, but especially to the electric utilities. These are costs that have been prudently incurred by utilities to serve their consumers but cannot be recovered if the consumers choose other electricity suppliers. Estimates of projected stranded costs range from a low of $10 to $20 billion to a high of $500 billion. Utilities are looking for ways to mitigate stranded costs, and regulators are evaluating who should pay them.

Stranded cost issues will significantly impact the evolution of competitive power markets around the country. Competition will likely lower electricity prices in many areas, but, according to a report from the Energy Information Administration (EIA), many short-term savings may be offset if state authorities mandate full recovery of stranded costs. In the absence of stranded cost recovery, electricity prices are expected to fall over the short term relative to where they would have been under traditional cost-of-service regulation. With 100% stranded cost recovery, competitive prices would differ little from regulated prices over the short term

In the long term (out to 2015) prices will decline if efficiency improvements or other cost reductions result from competitive pressures. EIA's short-term projections estimate price reductions due to competition at 8 to 15% without stranded cost recovery, including price reductions already seen from limited wholesale competition, producers' preparations for retail competition, and actions already taken by regulators. Price changes would vary from region to region. Regions with very low power generating costs in the current regulatory environment—such as the Pacific Northwest, with its low-cost hydroelectric generating capacity, and the Upper Midwest, with its low-cost coal-fired generating capacity—could see short-term price increases. Without policy mandates for stranded cost recovery, U.S. suppliers could experience a total reduction in market value approaching $170 billion, and there could be a number of bankruptcies.

Strategies being considered would allocate the costs to ratepayers, shareholders, "wheeling" customers, taxpayers, and/or nonutility suppliers.

Ideas such as delaying the start of retail competition, charging exit fees to departing customers, reducing administrative and general costs, and discounting qualifying facility energy payments are being considered. They are likely to result in reductions of 25% or more in an at-risk utility's stranded costs. In Order 888, FERC suggested that stranded cost recovery should be allowed because it is critical to the successful transition to a competitive wholesale environment with open access to transmission capacity. Stranded costs would be recovered from departing wholesale customers.

Publicly owned utilities and rural electric cooperatives will also be affected by industry restructuring. In general, they have lower operating costs than IOUs, and most of them can sell electricity at a competitive price. However, with increased competition from IOUs and electricity marketing companies, publicly owned utilities and cooperatives may find that they need to lower costs, as well. Many of them are now reacting to competitive pressures by reducing staff and engaging in other cost-cutting activities. Although a few publicly owned utilities have recently announced merger plans, theirs is not a significant merger trend when compared to IOUs. Publicly owned utilities can capture some of the same efficiencies of a merger by sharing resources and forming mutual-aid programs.

Objections to IOU merger plans have been raised by some publicly owned utilities who contend they result in unnecessary consolidation of generation capacity and create excess market power. One notable point of contention is the debate over private-use funding mechanisms. In the regulated environment, public power companies were able to use tax-exempt financing to fund investments serving their territories. Investor-owned utilities are concerned that if such privileges are extended to public power entities in a deregulated environment, the public power systems will gain an unfair operating advantage.

ISOs

The concept of an independent system operator (ISO)—an entity that will independently manage a transmission grid owned by one or more electric generation companies—is growing in importance. ISOs are considered by most parties to be a key component for achieving effective wholesale competition. One of the most important duties of an ISO in a deregulated marketplace is providing nondiscriminatory access to all suppliers to the transmission grid. Several ISOs are already operating in the U.S., and others are in various stages of development.

Properly designed ISOs can improve transmission system efficiency by incorporating market-oriented strategies and by establishing a single regional transmission tariff for all users. Many utilities have not yet joined an ISO, however, meaning that unified coverage is still several years off. Nonetheless, the nationwide importance of reliable and secure electricity transmission service will likely overcome regional resistance and ensure the development of ISOs across the U.S.

Power marketing

In addition to the activities of electric utilities, power marketers—companies that buy and then resell electric energy and transmission and other services from traditional utilities—are emerging as new players in the industry. Of the more than 3,000 electric utilities in the U.S., almost two-thirds do not have generating assets. As a result, more than half of the electricity that ultimately reaches end-use customers is purchased on a wholesale basis from other utilities and nonutilities.

Of the companies currently dominating the power marketing landscape, the majority are familiar names from the electric or natural gas industries, or both. These companies are using their industry knowledge and expertise to seek out profits in this developing landscape. Many of the top electricity marketers are also among the top natural gas marketers (Figs. 7-4 and 7-5).

Analyzing wholesale and retail electricity transactions results in several broad conclusions.

- The historical tendency for consumers to pay a premium for assured electricity supplies—firm power—has continued through the early days of competition. Correspondingly, non-firm power purchases are priced lower

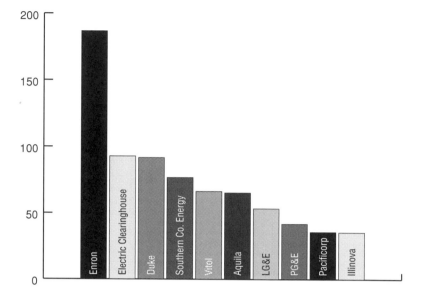

Fig. 7-4. Top Power
Marketers, 1997

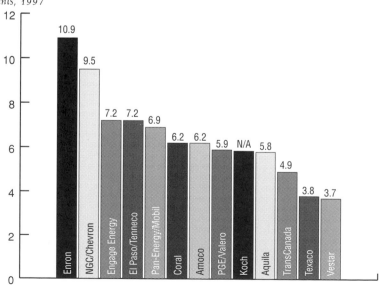

Fig. 7-5. Largest North
American Natural Gas
Merchants, 1997

- The firm power premium is expected to continue for the foreseeable future, even as trading practices change and evolve. Existing long-term contracts incorporating premium prices will probably be extended, but will eventually expire as markets mature
- Industrial customers have benefited the most from the opening of electricity markets, paying retail prices approximately equal to wholesale prices for firm power
- Stimulating power marketing growth, electricity spot markets are operating at several sites across the country. Power marketers and some electric utilities are using spot markets as an alternative source of wholesale power
- The California-Oregon Border (COB) and the Palo Verde switchyard are two of the largest electricity trading centers at this time. Electricity futures contracts—new financial instruments that help traders manage the risks in electricity trading—were started at COB and Palo Verde in March 1996. Two new sites were added in 1998, one into the Cinergy transmission system and one into the Entergy transmission system. A fifth delivery point—the Pennsylvania-New Jersey-Maryland Power Pool—has also been approved

The New York Mercantile Exchange launched the Cinergy and Entergy futures contracts on July 10, 1998. First-day volumes totaled 939 contracts on the two systems. This compares with the March 29, 1996 first-day volumes at COB and Palo Verde of 1,221 contracts. NYMEX experience indicates that less than 1% of energy futures contracts will develop into physical delivery. Therefore, service to retail customers will not be affected by a utility participating in a futures market as a regional hub.

Electricity industry restructuring and open competition are forcing industry personnel to learn new lingo and business practices in order to succeed. The use of financial derivatives is assuming a greater role in energy companies' management strategies. Forwards, swaps, futures, options, caps, floors, and collars are all terms that industry participants must understand to prove profitable in the open market. These financial instruments will gain importance in mitigating stranded costs, providing information to make capacity and transmission investment decisions, and helping customers manage newly conferred risks.

Electric utility industry deregulation is a fluid phenomenon. With no previous experience in direct competition, there are bound to be system upsets and unusual events. One of the most significant transpired in the Midwest in June 1998. A number of factors conspired to place tremendous pressures on the wholesale electricity market. High temperatures, the loss of the Davis Besse Nuclear Power Plant in Ohio due to tornado-induced damage, and the unavailability of several other power plants in the region left several utilities short of power. The supply shortfall caused spot market electricity prices to spike as high as $7,000/MWh, from an average of about $30/MWh. Several utilities and some commodity traders lost millions of dollars during the trading turmoil, as they were forced to buy electricity at many times conventional rates. The market problem led to litigation.

FERC investigated the matter, to determine if any measures are needed to ensure "a responsible market" is maintained. Because the Midwest price spike corrected itself within 24 hours, its occurrence should not be used as evidence against deregulation. It merely highlights the "patchwork" nature of the electricity market and its varying levels of competition and limited transparency. Time and experience are expected to iron out the kinks and establish an efficient, responsive, reliable system.

Public opinion

Public opinion surveys completed by RKS Research and Consulting reveal some interesting contrasts before and after open competition in California, and between California and the rest of the nation.

For example, 81% of California residents were aware of deregulation, compared to 42% nationally. Although less clear about how competition will actually work, 75% of California residents supported the ability to choose their energy providers. They also expected significant savings—on average, a 14% savings, much greater than the guaranteed 10% rate cut. Utilities may have been at fault for inflating customers' savings expectations. Only 46% of

California residents reported receiving any information from their current providers about the major changes that were coming to the state's markets. Only one-third of those receiving information answered their questions. Another third felt the materials raised more questions.

California's savings expectations mirror national trends. New England electricity consumers reported anticipated savings of 20% in a similar research study, demonstrating the high expectations that utilities are expected to achieve.

More ominously, nationwide satisfaction scores at the end of 1997 declined in three of the four categories measured by RKS in its baseline survey addressing price, power delivery, and customer service. Only utility competence and integrity remained unchanged. Satisfaction levels showed the sharpest declines in the Northeast and in California—the two regions of the country where deregulation efforts are most advanced.

Despite the negative trends, the RKS study found some positive news for utilities wanting to sell products and services to residential customers. The majority of survey respondents support the idea of a single monthly bill that combines electricity, gas, water, and sewer and trash services. Customers also expressed interest in low-tech services such as electricians, appliance repair, heating and air conditioning, and plumbing offered in the name of their local utility.

Driving change

Factors motivating the changes occurring in the electric power industry include advancements in power-generating technology, legislative and regulatory mandates, and regional electricity price variations. Benefits from advancements in power-generating technology include:

- New advanced generators are cleaner and use less fuel
- Technological advancements have enabled generators to produce electricity at lower cost than utilities that use older fossil-fueled or nuclear-fueled steam-electric technologies

- The new generators can be built and put into operation quickly—sometimes as an alternative to utility capacity at existing central station plants

Legislation has been an important driver of change for the electric industry, just as it has been in the gas industry. The Public Utility Regulatory Policies Act of 1978 (PURPA) stipulated that electric utilities had to interconnect with and buy, at the utilities' avoided cost, capacity and energy offered by any nonutility facility meeting certain criteria established by the FERC. The Energy Policy Act of 1992 (EPACT) opened access to transmission networks and exempted certain nonutilities from the restrictions of the Public Utility Holding Company Act of 1935 (PUHCA). PUHCA broke up massive interstate holding companies and required them to divest their holdings until each became a single consolidated system serving a circumscribed geographic area. PUHCA permitted holding companies to engage only in business that was "essential and appropriate" for the operation of a single integrated utility, thereby practically eliminating the participation of nonutilities in wholesale electric power.

In 1996, FERC issued Order 888 which opened transmission access to non-utilities, thereby establishing wholesale competition, and Order 889 which requires utilities to establish electronic systems to share information about available transmission capacity.

Capacity needs

Despite slower-demand growth, about 400 GW of new generating capacity will be needed by 2020 to meet growing demand and to replace retiring units. Many older fossil plants with higher generating costs will likely be retired in the next few years. Between 1996 and 2020, 52 GW (51%) of existing nuclear capacity and 73 GW (16%) of fossil-steam capacity are expected to be retired. Before the advent of natural gas combined-cycle plants, fossil-fired base load capacity additions were limited primarily to pulverized-coal steam units; however, efficiencies for combined-cycle units are expected to approach 54% by 2010, compared to 38% for coal-steam units, with construction costs only about one-third those of coal plants.

Before building new capacity, utilities are expected to use other options to meet demand growth—life extension and repowering of existing plants, power imports from Canada and Mexico, and purchases from cogenerators. Even so—assuming an average plant capacity of 300 MW—a projected 1,344 new plants with a total of 403 GW of capacity will be needed by 2020 to meet growing demand and to offset retirements. Of the new capacity, 85% is projected to be combined-cycle or combustion turbine technology fueled by natural gas or both oil and gas. Both technologies are designed primarily to supply peak and intermediate capacity, but combined-cycle technology can also be used to meet base load requirements.

Convergence

8

a s deregulation pushes the natural gas and electricity industries together, any and all tools are helpful in the quest for profits in the open market.

Companies that deal in both natural gas and electricity have a big advantage over companies that deal only in electricity or natural gas. Diverse companies have the ability to maximize profits from their products. Gas can be stored until prices rise to a certain level, or it can be moved to another part of the country where demand is higher and gas is more valuable. It can also be burned to create electricity under peak power conditions to turn a tidy profit. These companies have more options and therefore a greater chance to create profits, regardless of the economic or weather conditions.

As in all competitive businesses, the quest for profits drives the convergence trend. As the wheels of deregulation continue to turn, so too do the wheels of convergence.

Giant one-stop energy providers have mushroomed as deregulation of the U.S. electric power business unfolds. The Btu convergence spawned by deregulation of first the gas, and now the electric power industries, is at the heart of an unprecedented series of proposed and completed mergers between natural gas pipeline/distribution companies and electric utilities. A stream of mergers, partnerships, alliances, and other cooperative agreements is running rampant throughout the industry—the brand new Btu industry, that is. As industry and corporate lines continue to blur, we need scorecards to keep track of the players. Two businesses that were stable, regulated industries are becoming vibrant competitive fields with lots of action and movement.

Mergers and acquisitions

Gas and electric companies seeking to join forces are experiencing growing pains along the way, as regulators take a close look at the altogether new, converged Btu business sector that is emerging.

Convergence mergers between electric and natural gas companies have proliferated in the second half of the 1990s. Of the mergers and acquisitions announced between 1992 and the first half of 1998, 39% have involved an electric company and a gas company, according to Edison Electric Institute figures (Fig. 8-1). Investor-owned electric utilities see tremendous value—synergistic operations and savings as well as trading expertise—in convergence mergers. Convergence allows companies to move toward becoming complete

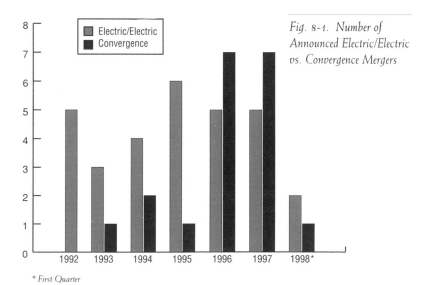

Fig. 8-1. Number of Announced Electric/Electric vs. Convergence Mergers

* First Quarter

energy service providers—an important attribute for the deregulated marketplace. This is further demonstrated when companies change names upon completion of the merger; often for national branding purposes. In fact, a majority of convergence mergers, as well as all of the completed electric-electric mergers in the late 1990s, involved name changes.

Number of Announced Electric/Electric vs. Convergence Mergers

The majority of convergence mergers involve local distribution companies (LDCs) as well as gas marketers and gas pipeline companies. Through their connections with the pipelines, distribution companies purchase, distribute, and resell gas to customers. Not only do LDCs complement the energy needs of customers by offering a combination of energy products, they also provide complementary cash flow patterns for the new company. Because residential customers who use gas heat in the winter may use electricity to run air conditioners in the summer, more predictable cash inflows are achieved in the merged companies. If the distribution company's service territory encompasses an area in which there are potentially new electric customers, an opening exists for obtaining additional customers. Also, further market penetration for diversified services and products can occur if the service territories between the electric utility and distribution company overlap.

Gas pipeline companies are typically larger than distribution companies and offer a broad array of services. They may include gas gathering and processing in addition to marketing and trading functions. Pipeline accessibility to supply and transportation of natural gas often can complement gas generation facilities of the electric utility. Many gas companies have established marketing, trading, and business risk-management skills as a result of deregulation in the natural gas market.

Convergence can provide electric utilities with experienced employees and an operational infrastructure for trading. Trading skills are essential since it appears that electricity trading will be necessary to secure a commodity profit in the wholesale electricity business. Consequently, pipelines make ideal partners. By combining with a gas pipeline company, an electric utility may be able to procure diversified fuel inputs at lower costs and with lower risks.

Furthermore, in some cases, convergence mergers are appealing due to the lack of regulatory approval needed. In a case where FERC approval is needed, the process slows. With no approvals needed, convergence mergers have been completed in as little as six weeks; under a regulatory approval process, an electric-electric merger can take about two years.

While the term "convergence" has traditionally been used in the electric industry to define an electric utility merging with a gas company, it has recently been extended to describe combinations of electric companies with telephone, security, and cable companies. The wires are considered the convergence.

Most merger and acquisition activity consists of friendly combinations of investor-owned electric companies that jointly recognize the benefits in consolidating operations. While hostile acquisition attempts have occurred in the 80s and 90s, no hostile takeover has been completed thus far. In recent years, they have either been withdrawn—or turned friendly.

In 1997, CalEnergy withdrew its offer to buy New York State Electric & Gas after a two-month battle. In 1995, PECO attempted an unsolicited acquisition of PP&l Resources. This failed due to heavy local opposition. When Western Resources originally attempted a hostile take-over of Kansas City Power & Light, it was rebuked. Negotiations then became friendly, and in March 1998, Western Resources and KCPL agreed to a restructuring of their merger agreement.

Utilities also are acquiring companies that complement their distribution network, including businesses such as home security, cable, telecom, and water. In order to be successful in the competitive environment, utilities are choosing industries with the same fundamental core business characteristics as electricity to achieve synergies.

Mergers and acquisitions are not the only way to achieve synergies and cost savings. Alliances, partnerships, and joint ventures are often attractive alternatives. Electric utilities are increasingly joining forces and combining their marketing efforts to establish strategic alliances with other industries, such as natural gas and telecommunications. These relationships avoid the costs associated with merger and acquisition activity as well as the cumbersome approval process involved. In fact, creative combinations can involve teaming up with other investor-owned electric utilities in search of increased revenues and earnings. These creative ventures all share one common goal— to accelerate growth and increase shareholder value.

Ramifications

Convergence has ramifications for finance, development, engineering, and operations. Survival requires a thorough understanding of these ramifications, plus the prerequisite strengths of a talented team and a long-term corporate commitment to a growth plan. Risks of failure are high. New strategies are needed to produce rewards adequate to justify the risks. As in the past, companies that are innovative, aggressive and persistent, with a long-term business approach, will succeed.

Selling energy and related services by the Btu promises to be the largest competitive U.S. enterprise spawned by the wave of deregulation that started in the 1970s.

With annual revenues approaching $300 billion, the Btu business will be larger than either airlines or telecommunications. As is frequently noted, electricity is the largest industry ever to be deregulated. As a result, regulators are being extra cautious to ensure that they don't create a monster of anti-competitive giants with the potential to dominate regional electricity markets.

Maximizing profits

Despite huge profit potentials down the road, making money by combining power and gas companies may prove elusive at first. This is due in part to the premium being paid by the acquiring companies and also because the market is so new that no one is certain of the best way to tap the potential profit. This explains the smattering of pilot programs and customer choice offerings utilities are using as they seek to find their way in the murky waters of deregulation.

The merger trend began in earnest in 1996 and the announcements continue to roll in as companies scramble to gather the resources necessary to become total energy providers. One big, unanswered question is how many of these monstrous energy companies can be winners in the deregulated market. Advertising and branding campaigns are popping up around every corner. Electric and gas companies in a monopoly structure didn't need to advertise very much; they had captive customers. As the doors of the markets open, these same companies are finding that to retain their current customers—and to capture new customers and market share—they need to advertise. As a result, everything from sporting events to cultural programs are being sponsored by utilities trying to establish a brand name. Advertising campaigns are becoming fixtures on radio and television, and in newspapers and magazines.

Power and gas marketing firms may become key players in the deregulated energy business of the future. Despite widespread expectations for the convergence of electricity and gas services held by energy marketers, most large energy users prefer to use a marketer specializing in gas to handle their natural gas needs, and a marketer specializing in power to deal with their electric power needs, according to a recent survey. Many business customers do not differentiate between marketers and their traditional utility energy suppliers. For instance, large energy users point to the importance of reliable energy supply, service dependability, and quality/reliability of fuel sources as the top three criteria they use to differentiate among power and gas marketers.

The challenge for facing energy marketers is familiarizing customers with their unique service offerings and encouraging customers to use and rely on them. e.g., some of the marketers' unique offerings—commanding market presence, fuel diversity, skill in using financial derivatives, and a record of successful risk management—tend to be placed at the bottom of the list of characteristics that energy users use to differentiate among the different power and gas marketers.

One characteristic—financial strength—does apparently impress energy users. They say that when financial strength is summarized in a credit rating (such as those published by the major rating agencies) these ratings would play an important role.

Another study found that national chains such as Wal-Mart and other large retailers, plan to reduce the number of energy companies they deal with. Rather than buying from the local utility at each site, these large consumers plan to narrow their purchasing to a handful of national players once markets open. This will simplify billing and payment functions and allow these companies to use their energy purchase volumes to negotiate more favorable rates.

The gas precedent

The deregulation of natural gas preceded electricity in the move away from rate-based, cost-of-service regulation in the U.S., but the restructuring of the natural gas industry is not yet complete. In addition to fine-tuning the federal initiatives that started the process, the application of FERC Order 636—principles promoting competition and customer choice behind the city gate—is a very active arena. Also, implementation of FERC Orders 888 and 889 that started the restructuring of the wholesale bulk power market, is yielding innovations useful to the gas industry and to its regulators.

Although the gas and electricity markets have organizational and operational idiosyncrasies, the principles of a competitive market apply to both. Electric is emulating the gas industry model of function and service unbundling, and the elimination of the pipeline merchant function, for instance. The process of one industry learning from another is inevitable as electricity and natural gas come to be traded in a nearly unified energy market. As their markets merge, two once-distinct industries are becoming much more alike, each borrowing the best features of the other.

For natural gas, interaction with the lagging but more rapidly deregulating electric industry can provide cures to competitive imperfections that survived gas industry deregulation. The electricity industry's concept of ISOs, in particular, provides a model that the gas industry might use to remedy concerns about a competitive market for pipeline transportation capacity and associated services.

Another area in which the electricity industry has struck out on its own is use of the internet rather than the natural gas industry's proprietary electric bulletin boards for the exchange of and access to market information. One reason for this is that the power industry works with very short lead times, so the utilities have historically worked very closely with each other to share critical operating information. Transmission for power companies is reserved at least a day ahead of delivery, but hourly adjustments to energy schedules are possible and common. This brought about the development of the Open Access Same-Time Information System (OASIS).

The gas industry is also looking at ancillary services, with ideas such as sales of fuel gas, "parking", loaning, and other services coming from pipeline companies—ideas that might not be provided by a natural monopoly. There is a trend among pipelines to identify as many current functions as possible as "enhanced" or "value added" services and charge separately for them. Much of this effort is motivated by the formation of a class of service providers called "hubs" or "market centers". This effort can help make the market flexible and responsive to customers' needs. There is also the possibility of it hurting the market by creating unwarranted layers of cost.

Both natural gas and electricity industry players are struggling to compete on a "level playing field" with unregulated competitors.

Merchant competition

Merchant power plant projects are springing up around the country in anticipation of open market competition. Developers are betting that these new projects will be more competitive than existing, less-efficient capacity in spot markets. Some companies are buying existing utility assets with plans to operate them as merchants and make money on the margin. Merchant facilities are almost unanimously gas-fired sites. (The merchant phenomenon is discussed in detail in chapter 12.)

Not all existing generation will be uncompetitive, however. Some companies are repowering existing generation capacity to make it competitive. Replacing or renovating existing plants will be a huge market in the U.S. in the next decade. Of the 700,000 MW of capacity in the U.S., it is estimated that up to two-thirds will be replaced by 2010.

Long-term sales contracts are disappearing, and so are long-term fuel contracts. Developers operating in a merchant market will not be able to commit to a fixed-price, long-term fuel supply agreement. Instead, they will need a long-term relationship with a fuel supplier willing to accept price risks, possibly taking an equity position in the electric project.

Power and fuel infrastructure projects are more frequently being developed in tandem, with one supporting and justifying the other. A few fuel companies have historically been leaders in the global independent power business. These companies are finding partners increasingly willing to become power developers. Aligning with fuel companies is a logical direction for power companies to take—especially in merchant power markets, where low fuel costs mean the difference between profitability and bankruptcy.

The industry can expect more acquisitions, mergers, and joint venture partnerships between power companies and fuel suppliers. Fuel companies will become significant equity sponsors, possibly emerging as the dominant players of the IPP industry's next decade.

For large energy conglomerates or small developers, efficiency is the name of the game in competition. In the big picture, efficiency will be realized, and the worst producers will get eliminated.

A growing number of electric utilities are launching new businesses based on operating, and even owning, large industrial and commercial power plants.

It remains to be seen exactly how the trend toward convergence of electricity and natural gas will finally shake out, but it has emerged as a popular business strategy, and the markets seem to find it a savvy stance. Whether or not the truly blended Btu business will ever really exist, the lines between these two industries have certainly faded. They may well eventually be eliminated.

Power Plant Basics

9

e lectric power plants, like other manufacturing facilities, process raw materials into products, generally with some waste products. For power manufacturers, the main product is electricity. Waste materials, depending on the fuel used, can include ash and emissions to air, water, or soil.

Electricity is an unusual product in that it is both invisible and dangerous to handle. One difficulty that is peculiar to the power industry is that electricity generally cannot be stored. It must be generated as needed.

In generating plants, fuel is converted into heat energy, then into mechanical energy, and finally into electrical energy. Fuel is burned to heat water, making steam, which turns an engine or turbine, which runs a generator. Figure 9-1 illustrates the steps involved in energy conversion to power.

Fig. 9-1. Schematic Diagram of Energy Conversion

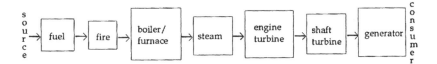

The most common fuels are fossil fuels, particularly coal, oil, and natural gas. They are burned in a steam boiler, which emits steam to run a steam engine or turbine that is connected by a drive shaft to an electrical generator. Nuclear power plants are steam electric plants in which a nuclear reactor takes the place of a furnace. The heat comes from the nuclear reaction, called fission, rather than from burning fossil fuels. The equipment used to convert that heat power is basically the same as that in an ordinary steam-electric plant. Figure 9-2 illustrates the connection of these basic pieces of equipment.

The boiler in the drawing is a device for turning water into steam. The steam jet issuing from the spout spins the fan (turbine) and also the generator. In the drawing the simplest example of boiler and turbine are shown. Actual power generation equipment, obviously, is much more complicated.

To most people the process of generating electricity is mysterious, but the actual process is easy to understand. As shown, the generator consists of

Fig. 9-2. The Process of
Electricity Generation

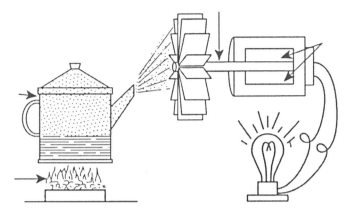

a little bar magnet spinning inside a stationary coil of wire. This is a simple example, but generators really are made of a magnet rotating inside a coil of wire. As the magnetic field emanating from the ends of the magnet moves across the turns of wire in the coil, an electric current is set up in the wire. By winding a large number of turns of wire into a ring, or doughnut, the current set up in each succeeding turn is added to the current set up in previous turns, and a much more powerful current is produced.

It may be surprising that so simple a process leads engineers to create massive, complicated electric power generating plants. The reason real power plants are more complicated is that our little plant in the illustration has an extremely low efficiency rating—close to 0%. Today's complicated power plants can approach 60% efficiency. Natural gas facilities boast the highest efficiency ratings. The higher the efficiency rating, the more electricity generated from the same quantity of fuel.

Engineers are constantly working to improve equipment efficiencies, because fuel is the number one expense of power generation. Today's coal-fueled power plants use less than one-third as much coal to generate the same amount of power as the power plants of the 1920s and 1930s.

In the teakettle illustration, much of the heat from the fuel escapes as hot air or hot water from the spout. The energy used to heat the water or air is wasted, reducing the efficiency of the process. In a power plant, there are two primary ways to recapture and use heat that would be lost in a simple-cycle process, such as the one in the illustration.

The first process is called *cogeneration*—the combined production of electricity and another form of energy such as heat or steam, all at the same time. The steam from the teakettle that turns the turbine would be captured in a cogeneration plant and used for industrial processes, or for heat. District heating systems—using steam to heat water running through pipes in buildings—are very popular in Europe. Using cogeneration steam for industrial needs, such as cooking soup in preparation for canning, are popular in the U.S.

The second method is called *combined-cycle generation*—producing electricity from otherwise lost waste heat exiting from a gas turbine. The heat is routed to a conventional boiler or to a heat-recovery steam generator for use by a steam turbine to produce *more* electricity. Adding equipment to convert an older fossil-fired power plant from a simple-cycle to combined-cycle process is a popular way to make older generating plants more efficient.

Fuels

The amount of heat energy contained in a fuel is measured in Btus. (A Btu is approximately equal to the amount of heat emitted by a kitchen match. It is enough heat to raise the temperature of one pound of water by 1°F. e.g., one ton of coal holds approximately 25 million Btus.)

Coal is the most popular fuel for electricity generation in the U.S., accounting for 31%. Natural gas is close behind at 27%. Due to fuel expense changes and emissions restrictions, cleaner burning natural gas has gained much popularity in the past few years and now accounts for most of the new construction in electric power plants. Oil is the third most popular fuel for power generation, accounting for 19%, followed by nuclear at 10%. Other fuels, such as wind, solar, and biomass, account for the remaining 13% (Fig. 9-3).

Fig. 9-3. Total U.S. Energy Production, 1996

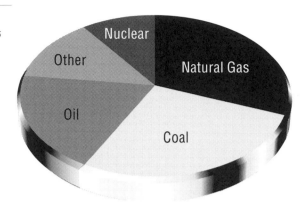

Loads

As mentioned earlier, electricity cannot generally be stored, and this is one difficulty of electricity generation. How much electricity power plant customers need varies according to the time of day and the day of the week. It also varies according to seasons and weather patterns. How much electricity is needed at any time is called demand. To meet demand power producers generally use a base load generating plant—a plant that is kept running to satisfy much of the minimum demand (also called the minimum load). This type of plant runs at a fairly constant rate. Base load plants are usually the newest and most efficient power plants (therefore the least expensive to operate) a generator has available.

For high loads (called peak loads) generators bring the less-efficient power plants on-line to increase the amount of available electricity. Large systems also have plants that are termed intermediate load units, used when the load exceeds the capacity of the base load plants, with the peaking units used only when demand is at its very highest; e.g., intermediate units may be used on weekdays when industrial plants use a lot of power. During the hottest days of summer, loads will go even higher than that, making use of peaking plants necessary. Any extra electricity-producing ability that an electricity generating system has beyond that peak demand is called reserve or standby capacity.

Transmission

Although some of the electricity generated at a power plant is used to run the plant's lights and systems, most of it needs to go somewhere else to be used. That is where transmission and distribution (T&D) come in.

The main components of a transmission and distribution system include a switchyard, transmission lines, a substation, and distribution lines (Fig. 9-4).

Fig. 9-4. T&D System Components

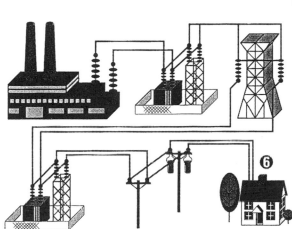

T&D system components

As seen in the illustration, the switchyard is generally sited right next to the power generation facility. The switchyard receives electricity from the power plant and directs it to the transmission lines. The switchyard is a junction connecting the T&D system to the power plant. The major electric lines are called the power grid. The grid is essential in times when customers need more power than a particular power plant is producing. It allows continuous flow and shifting of power from one area to another to ensure adequate power for customers at all times.

Transmission lines are sets of electricity conductors (wires) insulated from each other and from the towers that support them. They provide the path for electricity to be delivered to customers. Conductors—materials such as copper, silver, or copper-plated aluminum or steel—offer little resistance to the flow of electricity. Transmission lines carry electricity from the switchyard to substations and connect substations to provide alternate routes for the electricity.

When substations receive electricity from the transmission lines and switch it, they also regulate the voltage before passing it on to distribution lines, which carry the electricity to customers. This is because transmission lines carry high voltage—or highly concentrated electricity—from the power plant to the substation, and the distribution lines carry lower voltage electricity, which is suitable for customer use to businesses and residences in the area surrounding the substation. Transmission lines are those that can be seen running through the countryside, attached to big metal towers. Distribution lines are the much smaller and lighter weight lines that run up and down your block on wooden poles. The electric line that brings electricity from the pole to your home is also a distribution line.

The transmission system has three major parts—conductors, structures, and insulators. Conductors are the transmission system's electricity carrying wires. The structures are the poles or towers that hold the conductors. The insulators are devices used to hang the conducting wires from the structure.

Transmission lines have some resistance to the flow of electricity, which causes some power losses. The higher the voltage in a conducting electricity line, the less resistance, and therefore the less electricity wasted. This is why transmission lines that often carry electricity over long distances between power plants and substations are high voltage. Lower voltage distribution lines generally run only across short distances. The higher the voltage in an electric line, the more distance needed between the wire and the pole (or tower) holding it. The higher the voltage, the more insulators you see on the transmission structures.

The distribution system can be strung overhead or buried underground. In an overhead system, the power is delivered through wires strung from pole to pole. In underground systems, the cables buried run through conduits or ducts. Both types of distribution systems generally use most of the same components. Overhead systems are more common because they are less expensive to build and maintain.

When electricity enters a distribution system from the substation, it is at a voltage higher than that used in your home. The power passes through a distribution transformer to drop the voltage once again before the electricity is suitable for consumer use. Distribution transformers can be seen on residential power poles. They look like big metal cans with bushings on the top.

The entire electricity system we have been discussing can be seen illustrated in Figure 9-5.

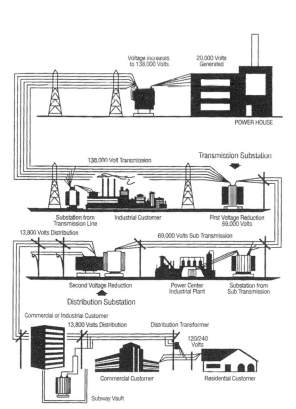

Fig. 9-5. The Electrical Supply System

Electricity originates at the electricity generating facility (termed a "power house" in the illustration). It moves to the switchyard, where its voltage is boosted for transmission. Once it is moved to where customers are located, the electricity passes through substations where its voltage is reduced. It continues through distribution lines to the distribution transformer, which reduces its voltage to residential rates. The final leg of its journey is through the distribution lines to residential and business customers.

Power Generation Technologies

10

t he workhorse of the natural gas-fired power generation industry is the gas turbine. These machines have found great popularity due to their high efficiency ratings, quick installation times, and low facility expense. Gas turbines of all makes and sizes are available to satisfy any market opportunity. Manufacturers are almost continuously announcing new models and various improvements in this technology (Figs. 10-1, 10-2, and 10-3).

Common to all these new turbines are claims of high efficiency and low emissions when compared to their predecessors. Manufacturers of small industrial turbines and utility-scale combined-cycle units boast of their heat rates and NO_x emission figures. High efficiency and low emissions will no doubt remain top priorities in the coming years, spurring even higher performance goals. Some of the more interesting innovations have been developed in the Department of Energy's (DOE) Advanced Turbine Systems (ATS) program. The use of devices such as recuperators, intercoolers, lean premix combustors, catalytic combustors, and brush seals are all advancing gas turbine design.

Fig. 10-1. A GE MS9001FA gas turbine, with the case open. This is a large gas turbine, suitable for use in an electric utility generating station.

Fig. 10-2. The rotor and part of the hybrid burner ring combustor of a Siemens 60-Hz heavy-duty gas turbine. This model V84.3A achieves an output of 170 MW, with a simple-cycle efficiency of 38% and a combined-cycle efficiency exceeding 58%. Emissions are less than 25 ppm when firing natural gas.

Fig. 10-3. The Rolls Royce Industrial Trent aeroderivative gas turbine at the Whitby Cogeneration Limited Partnership plant in Ontario, Canada.

Three areas in particular—cooling system design, materials development, and thermal barrier coatings—have experienced significant advances. Combined-cycle efficiencies exceeding 60% are expected for utility turbine systems generating around 400 MW per unit. For industrial turbines of less than 20 MW, a 15% improvement in simple-cycle efficiency is mandated.

To achieve the conflicting goals of higher efficiency—which requires higher firing temperatures—and lower NO_x emissions—which require lower combustion temperatures—ATS gas turbine gas-path cooling systems had to be improved. This allows manufacturers to increase firing temperatures by about 200°F for a higher efficiency with no increase in combustion temperature, limiting NO_x formation. Major turbine manufacturers such as Siemens Westinghouse, Allison Engine Company, and Solar Turbines are participating in the DOE program.

Hand-in-hand with cooling technology developments are advances in materials for turbine components that are essential to reaching performance goals. Materials development has benefited greatly from aircraft materials research and development. For instance, single crystal-nickel superalloys common in today's high-temperature aircraft turbines, are now working their way into component designs for land-based gas turbines. Some manufacturers are also experimenting with ceramics in turbine blades to allow an increase in the rotor inlet temperature that leads to fuel efficiency improvements and power upgrades.

Despite all these advances, however, limitations remained as close as the metal surfaces of the turbines. They would not be able to withstand the inlet firing temperatures for very long without a thermal barrier coating-æcoatings that provide insulation and protection between the combustion gases and the metal substrate.

Natural gas research, development, and demonstration programs at the DOE have been receiving record levels of funding—$246 million allocated in fiscal year 1999, up from $209 million in fiscal year 1998. The ATS program received more than $56 million for 1999. The DOE fossil energy budget contains an annual total of $115 million for natural gas programs and the Energy Research budget contains an annual total of $13 million for natural gas programs.

DOE's ATS program includes funding for microturbine and small industrial scale turbine development as well. Microturbines are small, high-speed turbines that typically put out less than 300 kW (about 400 horsepower). Industrial turbines generally generate less than 20 MW. Both technologies offer opportunities for distributed power generation—installing small power generation units near a site where the electrical power is needed, such as an office building, a hospital, or an industrial facility. They also offer the possibility of cogeneration for large-scale customers who want to generate their own electricity with a system that also supplies heating, cooling, dehumidification, process steam, or drying.

Industrial Potential

Industrial customers represent between 5% and 10% of a utility's customer base, but these customers consume the largest share of the natural gas pumped through the pipelines of every gas utility. This small percentage of customers use about half of the total natural gas consumed in the U.S. annually. They use natural gas in manufacturing and processing. Natural gas may be used to make steam and electricity, to compress air or other gases, and to heat and cool buildings and materials. Industrial customers provide a reliable base for gas sales, but the fuel must be cost competitive—these customers use gas to create products that must be sold at a profit. If fuel costs increase, it increases the cost of their products.

Many products aimed at these customers are being created or improved. They include improved reciprocating natural gas engine systems and hybrid gas-electric systems to power machinery, pump water, provide refrigeration, and compress air or other gases. Reciprocating engines have been used to compress natural gas in pipelines since the 1940s, so they hardly qualify as a new technology. But improvements of late include computerized control systems, new options, smarter equipment configurations, waste heat recovery, and use of these engines to avoid high prices for peak power.

New natural gas turbines that are smaller and simpler than those installed in electric utility plants are commercially available. Small units can be used for on-site power generation, and also for refrigeration, air compression, and other industrial energy needs (Figs. 10-4 and 10-5). Microturbines and larger industrial size turbines show great promise for distributed power generation. They allow industrial customers to operate their own on-site power plants or to build an on-site plant and hire the local utility or other qualified service provider to run it for them. These units are also used to generate electricity at sites where the electricity grid is not available, such as remote locations or on construction-sites. Microturbines can also provide electricity locally for office buildings, hospitals, supermarkets or other institutions with heavy electrical loads in air conditioning and lighting. Natural gas turbines are also used for cogeneration.

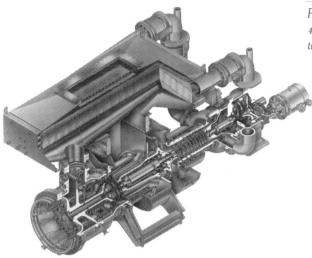

Fig. 10-4. Solar Turbine's 4.2 MW Mercury 50 gas turbine.

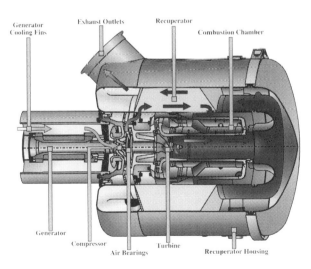

Fig. 10-5. Capstone's 30 kW Microturbine is compact, lightweight and multi-fueled for use in stationary or vehicular applications.

Generator Cooling Fins

Exhaust Outlets

Recuperator

Combustion Chamber

Generator

Compressor

Air Bearings

Turbine

Recuperator Housing

Fuel cells

Another priority in natural gas research programs is fuel cell development. Fuel cells convert hydrogen, natural gas, or methanol directly into electricity and heat using a chemical reaction. No combustion of fuel takes place, so fuel cells are favorable to the environment because they have virtually no pollutant emissions. Each contains three active components—two electrodes, over which the fuel and oxidant are passed, separated by an electrolyte. Fuel cells are named for the type of electrolyte they use between the electrodes. There are four types: Proton exchange membrane (PEM), molten carbonate (MCFC), solid oxide (SOFC), and phosphoric acid (PAFC).

PEM fuel cells operate at a comparatively low temperature (about 200°F). This gives them the advantage of quick start-up and makes them well suited for transportation applications. They may also be used in residential and commercial buildings. The preferred fuel for this particular technology is pure gaseous hydrogen, but phosphoric acid fuel cells are the closest to a commercial reality. They are already being used at hospitals, nursing homes, office buildings, schools, utility power plants, and on military bases.

MCFCs operate at an average temperature of 1,200°F. High temperatures do not favor the development of small fuel cells and so these cells are being used in power plant units from 250 kW to 10 MW. They can be used for base load distributed power and in industrial and commercial applications, running on reformed natural gas or other hydrocarbons.

SOFCs operate at 1,800°F and are made of metal and ceramic parts with no liquids. They are expected to last longer than the other types of fuel cells, all of which use some form of liquid and are therefore subject to some form of corrosion. SOFCs will run directly on methane if there is enough steam present to prevent carbon formation. They are also used with reformed natural gas, as are the MCFCs.

There are many fuel options for fuel cells, and while it remains to be seen what the primary technology and fuel will be, it is highly likely that natural gas will gain market share through fuel cells once they become more commercially viable. As fuel cell technology further develops, it may become an important element in the converging electricity and natural gas industries.

The greatest potential for SOFC technology lies with integration into a gas turbine in SOFC/GT cycles, where efficiencies are being quoted as high as 70% to 75% and emission levels are very low. This type of system is still under development, with research and development to be expanded before pilot plants are built.

The American Gas Association first suggested steam reforming of natural gas for use in PAFC and PEM stationary power plants. The idea was adopted by International Fuel Cells (ONSI) for its first stationary phosphoric acid fuel cell demonstrations in the 1970s. ONSI still uses steam reforming of natural gas. PAFC and PEM systems use natural gas purified by catalytic hydrodesulfurization (a small amount of hydrogen is mixed with natural gas and then passed over a hot nickel or cobalt-molybdenum oxide catalyst). Any sulfur is hydrogenated to hydrogen sulfide and absorbed by a bed of hot zinc oxide. Gas from the reformer is then passed through more catalysts to reduce its carbon monoxide content to the low level required by the fuel cells. This technology is well proven, having been adapted from large industrial systems. To reduce the cost of fuel cell systems, researchers are working to reduce the size of the necessary reformer.

Fuel cell development costs have fallen dramatically in the past decade, but the fuel cell industry still needs government support while additional research and development is pursued. The technology shows great promise for stationary power, portable power, transportation, and space or military use. Fuel cells were first researched for use by NASA in the space program. This diversity of application bodes well for commercialization.

The total world market for fuel cells is estimated to exceed $80 million for 1998, and dramatic growth is anticipated. Worldwide revenues from fuel cells are expected to approach $4 billion in 2008, with an estimated compound average growth rate approaching 40% by 2010. The largest share is expected to go to PAFCs.

Several fuel cell technologies are being developed for large stationary applications in the 1 to 2 MW range, particularly PAFCs,

SOFCs, and MCFCs. PAFCs are the most commercially ready, with more than 100 units in operation already. Most of these are in cogeneration systems.

UltraFuelCells are a new technology that is being researched by the Department of Energy office of Fossil Energy through the Federal Energy Technology Center (Table 10-1). These cells will be able to deliver extremely high fuel-to-electric conversion efficiencies in power generation coupled with ultra-clean environmental performance. The proposed system offers the following major advantages:

- Unprecedented natural gas fuel efficiencies, targeting 80% lower heating value when gas turbine bottoming is used, or 70% lower heating value when a simple cycle is used
- Ultra-clean (non-combustion) technology, with excellent potential to provide a pure steam of CO_2 with virtually no other emissions
- Marketability in the power, industrial, commercial, and transportation sectors on both small and large scales
- Potential for reductions of greenhouse gas emissions and increased economic competitiveness

Table 10-1. Comparison of Simple Cycle UltraFuelCell and Alternatives

	LHV Efficiency	Size	Status
UltraFuelCell Simple Cycle	70%	50 kW-MWs	Conceptual
UltraFuelCell w/ Gas Turbine	80%+	200 kW-MWs	Conceptual
Fuel Cell/Turbine Concepts	70%	200 kW-MWs	Conceptual
Current Fuel Cell	40-60%	250 kW	Developing
Advanced Turbines	60%	400 MW	Developing
Modern Large Turbines	42%	50 MW	Commercial
Average Grid Technology	35%	Wide range	Commercial
Micro Turbine	25%	28 kW	Developing

The UltraFuelCell technology concept allows operating temperatures and the operating temperature window for a solid-state fuel cell stack to be optimized for the maximum benefit of a power plant system. This type of system uses multiple stages of solid-state stacks to cascade heat and higher operating temperatures to the next downstream fuel cell stage, avoiding expensive heat exchanger cooling steps (Fig. 10-6). This reduces thermal requirements and improves heat integration, resulting in a plant efficiency of 82% when using natural gas. The 10-year cost of coal for UltraFuelCells is $100/kW—an 80% reduction over today's system.

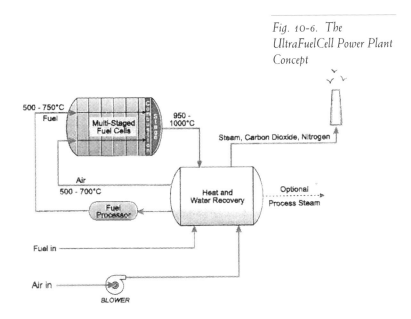

Fig. 10-6. The UltraFuelCell Power Plant Concept

Research and development is aimed at reducing the cost of fuel cell production. This is being accomplished through increased power density and output and through improvements in production technology. The amount of material used is also being reduced, making the cells smaller and lighter to decrease production costs. Fuel cell technologies generally use expensive electrolytes and catalysts so researchers are working to find ways to decrease the use of these materials. Power density of fuel cells has increased significantly in the past several years. High power density is important, particularly for portable power or transportation applications, where size and weight must be minimal.

The potential of combining fuel cells and gas turbines in a power plant are also being explored. A combination of high-temperature fuel cells and gas turbines could convert fossil fuels to electricity with an efficiency rate of around 70%. Today's best gas turbines flirt with the 60% efficiency mark.

Technologies that show potential for future cost reductions are drawing interest and research money from diverse companies, from power supply firms to automotive manufacturers, increasing the probability that fuel cells will eventually become a serious power generation option with significant market share.

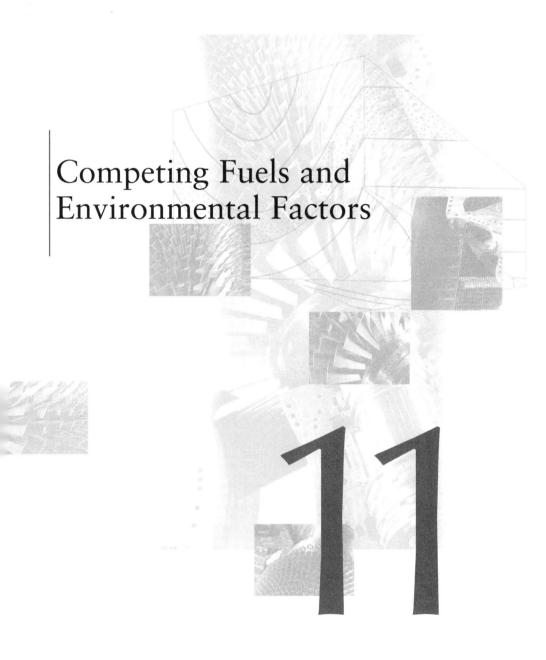

Competing Fuels and
Environmental Factors

11

C oal has long been the primary fuel for electricity generation, and it continues to be so today, with a bit more than 50% of total capacity. Nuclear generation is the number two source, holding steady at 17% of capacity as no new plants are being built in the U.S. Natural gas is third, ranking at 14%, but nearly all new capacity announcements plan to burn natural gas. Also, there is a trend under way to convert coal-fired facilities to natural gas. Oil and hydroelectric-powered generation fill out the list of top fuels (Figs. 11-1, 11-2).

Economic growth increases total energy consumption while technological advances cut it. Inflation and availability affect prices and use patterns as well. There is a long running trend of improvement in the efficiency of U.S. energy consumption that is expected to continue. Increasing demand for electricity is the major reason that energy consumption is expected to rise steadily in the future (Table 11-1).

Utility and nonutility fuel choices are very different. The largest portion of utility generation (57%) is coal-fired, but the largest portion of nonutility generation (52%) is gas-fired. A surprisingly large fraction of nonutility generation

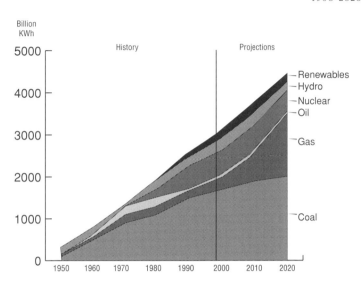

Fig. 11-1. Electricity Generation by Fuel, 1950-2020

Fig. 11-2. Electricity Generation by Fuel, 2020

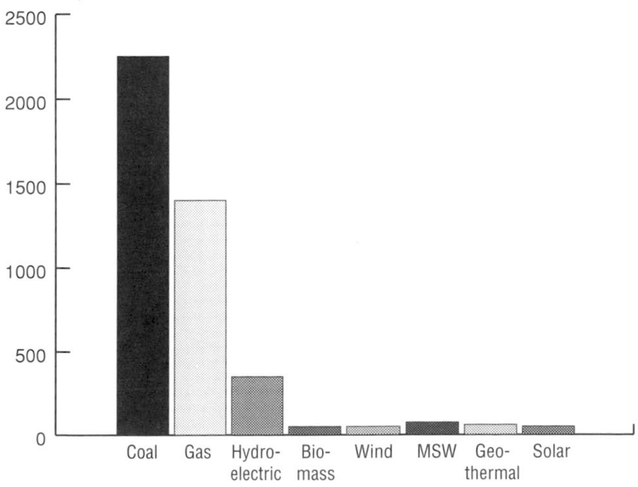

Table 11-1.
U.S. Energy Demand

Fuel	1996	1997 Trillion Btu	1998	% share (Total energy, 1998)
Oil	35,864	36,380	36,830	40.1
Natural gas	22,521	22,500	22,860	24.9
Coal	20,486	20,840	21,150	23.0
Nuclear	7,168	6,910	7,070	7.7
Hydro/other	3,933	4,120	4,020	4.4
Total	89,972	90,750	91,930	100.0

Source: *Oil & Gas Journal*

(14%), is fired by waste- and wood-fired power plants, compared to less than 1% for utility generation. These statistics highlight the opportunistic character of nonutility power producers, some of which have turned to unconventional fuels for lower-cost power generation.

Coal

Coal remains the leading fuel for electricity generation because of its long history as a low-cost fuel. Since the early 1980s, coal has experienced a steady decline in the price paid by electric utilities. The average real price of coal delivered to electric utilities in 1997 fell to $23.27/short ton, a 3% decline from 1996 and a 39.2% decline from 1987. The price decline is the result of several factors, including worker productivity increases, greater production, a shift in production methodology from underground to surface mining, and increased application of advanced technology (Fig. 11-3).

Coal production set an all-time record in 1997, reaching 1.09 billion short tons. It was the fourth consecutive year of 1 billion tons-plus production. The electric power industry set a corresponding coal consumption

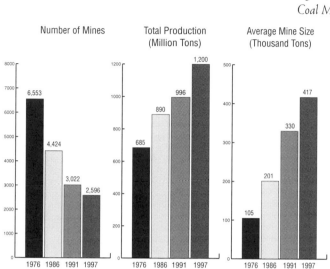

Fig. 11-3.
Coal Mining Statistics

record in 1997, using more than 900 million short tons at its power plants—æa 2.7% increase over 1996. The primary reason for the increased production is the increased importance of surface-mined Western coal, particularly the low-rank coal of the Powder River Basin in Wyoming. While Eastern coal production has remained steady at the 500-600 million short-ton level over the past 30 years, Western coal production has risen from less than 50 million tons in 1970 to more than 500 million tons in 1997. Powder River Basin coal accounts for the majority of this increase, as more and more utilities in markets near and far realize its economic and technical viability in a variety of boiler systems. Utilities are also benefiting from Western coal's low sulfur content, which helps them achieve compliance with SO_2 emission regulations under the Clean Air Act Amendments of 1990.

Coal mining productivity has substantially increased in the last 20 years, rising from 1.78 short tons per miner-hour in 1976 to 5.69 tons per miner-hour in 1996. There is a dramatic difference in productivity rates between surface and underground coal mines. Surface mines achieve productivity rates more than twice as high as underground mines—9.26 tons per miner-hour compared to 3.58 tons per miner-hour in 1996. Notably, however, both surface and underground coal mines have experienced similar gains in productivity; each rose about 200% over the past 20 years.

The productivity gains have been accomplished through the mining of thicker coal seams to take advantage of larger, more productive mining equipment, and through technological advances in underground mining machinery such as longwall systems.

Coal-fired power plants remain the lowest cost producers of electricity in the nation. Basin Electric Cooperative's 1,650 MW coal-fired Laramie River plant, for example, had total production costs of only $8.49/MWh in 1996, placing it first among all power plants. Remaining competitive and viable in the future, however, may depend on the state of environmental emission regulations, particularly for CO_2. If stringent CO_2 restrictions are imposed, coal-fired plants will be hard-pressed to retain their dominant generation position unless liberal emission credit trading programs are developed.

Natural gas

Natural gas is assuming a critical role in the U.S. electricity industry. The evolution and widespread popularity of high-efficiency combustion turbines and combined-cycles have placed greater pressure on the availability, distribution, and price of natural gas.

Domestic gas production has significantly increased in the last decade to meet this demand—to 18.96 tcf in 1997—but not as quickly as consumer demand, resulting in a 200% increase in imports over the same period. Imports comprised only 4.2% of consumption in 1986 but made up 12.8% in 1997. Canada, by virtue of its ample gas reserves, easy access to U.S. markets, and similar business philosophies, understandably accounts for all but a tiny fraction of imports. Although imports from Mexico are currently miniscule compared to Canada—15 bcf versus 2,880 bcf—growing use of natural gas in Mexico, economic development, and increased international trade may result in elevated Mexican import levels to the U.S. in the future (Fig. 11-4).

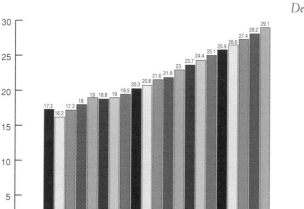

Fig. 11-4. Historic and Projected Natural Gas Demand

Increased U.S. natural gas production over the past few decades is more the result of a greater number of producing wells than increases in individual well productivity. A total of 304,000 wells were producing in 1997, compared to 117,000 in 1970, but productivity has fallen—from 433.6 mcf per day per well in 1970 to 157.3 mcf per day per well in 1997. Advanced technological techniques such as directional drilling are commonly being deployed to increase overall well productivity, but more wells will be needed to satisfy demand because the younger wells simply do not contain as much gas as the older wells.

Future growth of natural gas-fired generation depends on the availability of reasonably priced natural gas. Despite past predictions that natural gas reserves would be insufficient to support long-term demand, production is expected to rise consistently through 2020 and annual reserve additions are projected to keep pace with yearly consumption. Natural gas prices paid by electric utilities have remained relatively flat in the past decade, hovering around $2.00-$2.50 per mcf. These prices have encouraged power plant owners and developers to increase gas-fired generation and to commit to natural gas-fired capacity for new generation.

Also encouraging the selection of natural gas-fired generation are the evolution of high-efficiency combined-cycles, a drop in capital costs for new plants, and shorter construction schedules. Combined-cycle generating units based on the newest gas turbines can achieve efficiencies approaching 60%. This reduces fuel requirements per kWh, cuts generation costs, and reduces emissions per kWh compared to coal-fired units. Capital costs for combined-cycle power are now in the $400-500/kW range—significantly lower than the $900-1,000/kW capital costs for new coal-fired capacity.

Gas-fired combined-cycle plants can be brought on-line in less than two years—far more quickly than competing designs to shore up supply short-falls and to take advantage of near-term revenue opportunities.

Nuclear

Nuclear and hydroelectric power plants retain similar generation percentages, although there have been moderate fluctuations due to changing water runoff levels and higher nuclear capacity factors. Nuclear power currently accounts for about 18% of U.S. net generation, while hydroelectric power accounts for 10%. Both nuclear and hydroelectric power face somewhat uncertain futures (Fig. 11-5).

The number of operable commercial nuclear power units peaked at 112 in 1990. No new nuclear units have been ordered since 1978. Some 124 units were ordered but canceled prior to construction, between 1953 and 1997. Those that were shut down far outnumber the 107 units operable at the end of 1997. Several nuclear plants have recently been permanently shut down, including the 1,000 MW+ Zion plant in Illinois and the 35-year-old Big Rock Point plant in Michigan, either because they have reached the end of their useful lives or because they are not cost-competitive in a deregulated environment.

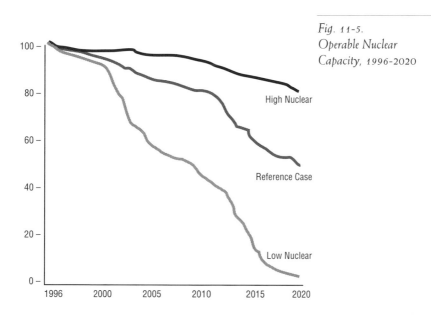

Fig. 11-5.
Operable Nuclear
Capacity, 1996-2020

Interestingly, however, nuclear power generation is enjoying increases in plant reliability, capacity factor, and overall plant competitiveness. Virginia Power's North Anna nuclear plant, for example, produced power for an average of $10.26/MWh in 1997, competitive with the best fossil plants in the country.

In one of the most significant demonstrations of how deregulation and open competition are affecting nuclear power generation, GPU Nuclear sold its Three Mile Island Unit 1 to AmerGen Energy Co. LLC (a joint venture between PECO Energy Co. and British Energy) in July 1998. This was the first sale of an operating nuclear power plant in the U.S. AmerGen says the purchase represents a strong statement that nuclear power plants are well positioned for competition in the electricity business. A number of other nuclear plants are beginning efforts to renew their operating licenses, convinced they can operate competitively for an additional 20 years. Nonetheless, it is estimated that 65 additional nuclear units will be retired between now and 2020, resulting in a steady decline in nuclear power's fraction of U.S. electricity production.

A final complicating factor for nuclear generation is waste disposal. The Department of Energy passed its January 31, 1998 deadline without opening a national spent-fuel storage facility, despite 16 years of preparation and more than $14 billion paid into the fuel management program by nuclear plants. On February 2, 1998, more than 50 states, state agencies, and municipalities filed a lawsuit against the Department of Energy to force it to develop a fuel storage plan in a timely fashion. Individual utilities are gradually following their lead and filing separate lawsuits.

Hydro

Hydroelectric power generation faces future uncertainty because of relicensing concerns. Growing opposition to hydroelectric power and its impacts on aquatic life, spawning routes, ecological patterns, land use, and recreational opportunities has made relicensing much less than automatic.

In 1997, hydroelectric opposition resulted in the first forced closure of an electricity-producing dam when FERC voted 2-1 to require the owner to remove the 3.5 MW Edwards Dam in Maine. FERC's reasoning was that the societal value of allowing several fish species to migrate further upstream outweighed the cost to remove the dam and the loss of electricity. It is unclear whether the decision represents an isolated instance or a harbinger of the hydroelectric power industry's demise. Contending that FERC overstepped its authority in the Edwards ruling, the National Hydropower Association (NHA) is leading efforts to get FERC to vacate its decommissioning order. Citing "negative consequences" if the order is allowed to stand, NHA and other industry associations believe that if the order is not vacated, their legal rights to contest future FERC orders could be in jeopardy.

In addition, the cost of licensing doubled between 1987 and 1996, highlighting the need for review and reform. A DOE report issued in September 1997 concluded that the hydroelectric power regulatory system has cost the nation billions of dollars in expenses and resulted in the loss of more than 1,000 MW generating capacity. A key reform action would be the establishment of a single agency with authority to regulate hydroelectric power projects. Since a number of agencies are currently involved in the licensing process—including the U.S. Fish and Wildlife Service, the Forest Service, the National Oceanic and Atmospheric Association, stage agencies, and FERC—achieving such a consolidation may be very difficult. FERC has already established an alternative process for hydroelectric relicensing that encourages flexibility and early participation by all stakeholders who wish to weigh environmental concerns against economic and social considerations. Resolving this process with any proposed legislation will be important in easing hydroelectric licensing hassles.

Renewables

Despite increased public awareness of, and technological development of non-hydroelectric renewable resources, their share of total electricity generation is still quite small. Only 2.3% of the nation's electricity is provided by non-hydroelectric renewables, up slightly from 1.8% in 1989. The main barrier to broader commercialization is higher cost of renewables compared to conventional generation sources. This is the result of renewables short history and its limited installed base (which currently precludes cost reductions afforded through mass production).

"Green power" programs in operation (or under development) around the country may provide a boost to non-hydroelectric generation. In these programs, utility customers pay an extra charge in their monthly electricity bills in exchange for renewables-based generation or guarantees that renewables-based generation is being used to offset generation from fossil-fired and nuclear capacity. In numerous opinion polls, U.S. consumers have expressed a strong willingness to pay extra for green power. Furthermore, more than 70% of respondents in one poll supported an increase in taxes on energy sources that pollute the environment and using those revenues to reduce existing payroll taxes. Respondents also supported a tax on air and water polluters, voicing slightly more support for this type of environmental "sin tax" than for taxes on cigarettes or liquor.

Green power programs are being developed not just by utilities in states where retail competition is already available (California) or soon to be available (Massachusetts, Pennsylvania), but also in states where deregulation legislation and open competition are still a way off (Colorado, Texas). Utilities nationwide have recognized that green power programs can raise revenues to support capital investments in renewable power plants and to provide experience with nontraditional forms of generation.

Certification programs are also being created to vouch for electricity products labeled as green power. The Center for Resource Solutions, a California nonprofit organization, oversees the Green-e branding program— a voluntary industry effort to set uniform standards for truthfulness in green energy labeling and advertising. The Green-e initiative was established to ensure—through independent third-party verification—that at least one-half of a green electricity product is renewable, with any remaining percentages containing less air pollution than an average California energy source.

Another tool providing a boost to renewables-based generation is federal tax credits. Currently set at $0.015/kWh, these credits can make renewable plants competitive with conventional generation. Perhaps benefiting most from these credits are wind turbine projects, whose capital costs have fallen to a level where the $0.015/kWh credit is enough to make them commercially attractive. The American Wind Association is supporting efforts for a five-year extension to the credits to facilitate greater renewables penetration in the U.S. energy mix.

Forecasts

Electricity demand has slowed in the past few decades from the lofty 7% per year growth rates experienced in the 1960s. Projected growth rates out to the year 2020 are estimated at little more than 1% per year by the Energy Information Administration's Annual Energy Outlook. The reduced growth rate is attributed to higher appliance and equipment efficiencies, utility demand-side management programs, and legislation promoting greater efficiency (Fig. 11-6).

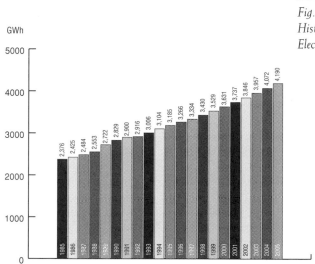

GWh

Fig. 11-6.
Historic and Projected
Electric Power Demand

Despite slower load growth, 403 GW of new generating capacity will be needed by 2020 to satisfy demand growth and replace retiring units. Between 1996 and 2020, 52 GW of current nuclear capacity and 73 GW of current fossil-steam capacity are expected to be retired. Of the new capacity, 85% is projected to utilize combined-cycle or combustion turbine technology fueled by natural gas or by natural gas and oil. Coal is expected to account for 49 GW, or 12% of the new capacity additions, while renewable energy will power the remainder. Despite the emphasis on natural gas and oil for new power plants, coal will remain the leading electricity fuel through 2020, although its share of generation is expected to fall to 49% in 2020. Natural gas-fired generation will experience the most dramatic increase, more than doubling from 14% of generation in 1997 to a whopping 33% in 2020 (Fig. 11-7).

Renewables-based generation, including hydroelectric power, is projected to rise only slightly in the EIA forecast, from 433 billion kWh in 1996 to 436 billion kWh in 2020. Almost the entire increase will come from renewable resources other than hydroelectric power, as a decline in conventional hydroelectric power is offset by a 34% increase in non-hydroelectric renew-

Fig. 11-7. Historic and Projected Non-traditional Gas and Electric Demand

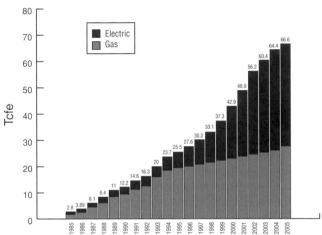

able power. Municipal solid waste (including landfill gas), wind, and biomass will account for the bulk of the renewables growth.

Environmental Issues

The number and the scope of environmental regulations have expanded from local to globally applied parameters in the last decade or so. This progression has brought with it the need to monitor, analyze, document, report—and comply on a whole range of elements. Electric utilities have demonstrated a commitment to meeting regulatory limits but must prepare for additional constraints that are sure to come.

Emissions are of great concern for most utilities. Threats of global warming, ozone alerts, and other news-making environmental issues such as acid rain, are causing governments the world over to enact legislation addressing emissions. The term broadly refers broadly to anything coming out of the stacks and into the atmosphere, but it really applies to all emissions, including anything going into the ground, water, or the air. Airborne emissions are more easily visible, and account for much more of the utility industry's total pollution, but land and water emissions are also regulated widely.

Emissions issues for an electric power plant tend to depend on the fuel it burns. Coal creates the most emissions among the popular fuels, yet is the most widely used electric power generating fuel, partially because it is abundantly available and relatively inexpensive to purchase, transport, and burn. However, its economics are being degraded by clean air regulations that limit emissions a power plant can make. Since coal makes the most emissions, coal-burning plants require the most equipment for reducing emissions in order to meet guidelines. This can add greatly to the cost of coal as a fuel (Fig. 11-8).

The Code of Federal Regulations is by no means leisurely reading, and remaining current on newly promulgated regulations takes commitment of time and focused attention. The complexity of the involved variables spawns

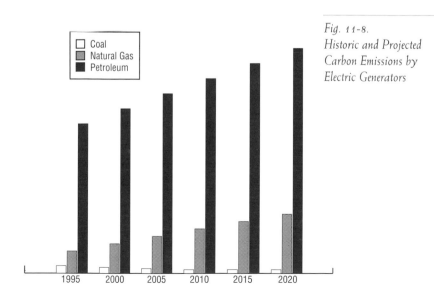

Fig. 11-8.
Historic and Projected Carbon Emissions by Electric Generators

confusion, misinformation and impatience as the wordy regulations are read—and hopefully—correctly interpreted. Avoiding fines for noncompliance is a strong motivator for accelerating the learning curve.

SO_2 and NO_x

Utilities successfully complied with Phase 1 of Title IV of the Clean Air Act Amendments (CAAA) of 1990. The U.S. Environmental Protection Agency's (EPA) acid rain program reduced SO_2 and NO_x emissions approximately 40% below the required levels. EPA reports that all 445 affected facilities demonstrate 100% compliance for both pollutants. These results were achieved after two years into the Title IV SO_2 and in the first year of the Title IV NO_x program.

The significance of these reductions is illustrated by several statistics. By 2010, under the currently regulatory limits in Title IV, national SO_2 emissions will be at the lowest level in nearly 100 years. Tons of SO_2 per kWh of total electric industry generation was 65% lower in 1995 than in 1970. By 2000, under the current regulatory limits in Title IV, NO_x emissions will decline by more than 2 million tons. Tons of NO_x per kWh of total electric industry generation was 35% lower in 1995 than in 1970.

When Phase 2 begins in 2000, SO_2 constraints on Phase I plants will be tightened and limits will be set for the remaining 2,500 boilers at 1,000 plants. With allowance banking, emissions are expected to decline from 11.6 million tons in 1995 to 10.2 million in 2000. Additional SO_2 emission reductions are expected in order to meet the 8.95 million tons per year cap set by the CAAA. Scrubber retrofits may be required to reach this level once banked credits are used (Fig. 11-9).

The NO_x reduction program involves two phases. Phase 1 (1996 to 1999) applied to dry-bottom wall-fired and tangentially fired boilers (Group 1) by using available control technologies. Phase 2 tightens the annual emissions limits imposed on the Phase 1 large, higher emitting plants and also sets restrictions on smaller, cleaner plants fired by coal, oil, and gas. Proposed Phase 2 reductions will achieve an additional decrease of 820,000

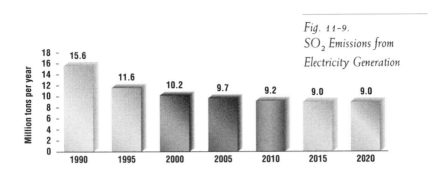

Fig. 11-9.
SO$_2$ Emissions from
Electricity Generation

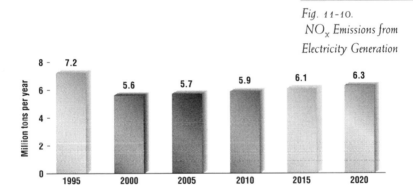

Fig. 11-10.
NO$_x$ Emissions from
Electricity Generation

tons of NO$_x$ annually (for a total of more than 1.5 million tons per year). Under current regulations, although NO$_x$ emissions are expected to decline between 1995 and 2000, an increase of nearly 0.7 million tons is predicted by 2020 due to increased coal use (Fig. 11-10).

Ozone and Fine Particulates

Also pressuring NO$_x$ and SO$_2$ emissions are revised standards EPA proposed in 1997 for ozone and particulate matter (PM) under the National Ambient Air Quality Standards (NAAQS) program. The new standards, effective in 2005, would result in many more U.S. counties designated as nonattainment zones for either or both ozone and PM. The proposed ozone standards add an eight-hour concentration limit to the existing one-hour standard, and the PM standards for the first time will include restrictions on the amount of fine particulate matter (less than 2.5 micron diameter, PM2.5) that can be in the air.

The ozone standards have aroused debate because of uncertainties regarding "ozone transport". Ozone transport occurs when emissions from one area drift downwind and, when combined with the local emissions of ozone precursors, may contribute significantly to the ozone concentration in the downwind area, i.e., Northeastern states allege that transfers from power plants in the Ohio Valley and the Midwest are causing them to exceed the ozone standard.

In 1997, EPA proposed that power plants in 22 states east of the Mississippi River reduce NO_x emissions by 85% by the summer of 2003 to address ozone concerns in the region. These reductions would be achieved through revisions to state implementation plans (SIPs). EPA contended that this action would reduce the amount of pollution transported to the Northeast.

The Alliance for Constructive Air Policy (ACAP) and the Electric Power Supply Association (EPSA) have raised objections to the EPA proposal. They contend that EPA significantly understated the economic impacts of the proposal and that certain provisions may be counterproductive by prohibiting the permitting of cleaner-burning power plants. ACAP has also put forth a relaxed NO_x-reduction proposal that would provide a smaller, but significant, drop in NO_x emissions while giving scientists more time to examine ozone transport.

The $PM_{2.5}$ standards are potentially troublesome to the electricity industry because of their restrictions on the finest particles. The critical point for power plant operators with respect to fine particulate matter lies in the fact that most $PM_{2.5}$ shows up downstream of the stack through the condensation of nitrates and sulfates. In other words, existing particulate matter control devices are effectively controlling *primary* fine particulate matter. Their Achilles heel is *secondary* particulate matter. Depending on the outcome of studies investigating the relationship between particulate matter and human health, tighter regulations for $PM_{2.5}$ precursors such as SO_2 and NO_x may be in the offing.

EPA will install 1,500 monitors around the country in the next few years to collect data regarding amount and speciation of ambient fine particulate matter. Because compliance deadlines for new ozone and particulate matter NAAQS do not occur until the middle of the next decade, data from these monitors will be available to guide implementation and to impact the next round of NAAQS reviews, which are mandated every five years by the Clean Air Act.

Mercury

EPA issued the long-awaited Utility Air Toxics Report to Congress in late 1997, concluding that although uncertainties in the analysis exist, on balance, mercury from coal-fired utilities is the hazardous air pollutant of greatest potential public health concern. Other toxics for which there were potential concerns (and uncertainties that need further study) included dioxins, arsenic, and nickel. EPA identified the highest emitters of mercury as coal-fired utility plants and municipal waste incinerators.

The same amount of mercury has existed on the planet since it formed. Its movement through the environment results from natural and human activities. Human activities most involved in emitting mercury into the air are the burning of mercury-containing fuels and materials and industrial processes. Mercury is eventually deposited from the air into water and land.

Human exposure to mercury occurs primarily through eating contaminated fish. Although serious neurological effects associated with high accidental levels of mercury exposure are well documented, no consensus has yet been reached on the effects of chronic consumption of low levels. EPA states that mercury is the most frequent basis for fish advisories, represented in 60% of all water bodies where advisories were issued. Furthermore, mercury advisories increased 28% between 1995 and 1996.

Despite finding no direct link between industrial mercury emissions and human health, and despite the current unavailability of a feasible mercury control technology for coal-fired power plants, there is a good chance EPA will limit mercury emissions in the near future. In fact, complaints from environmentalists—including health effects such as fetal damage, learning disabilities, and memory loss—recently resulted in EPA requiring the Tennessee Valley Authority to monitor mercury emissions from its 11 coal-fired plants.

EPA also recently required monitoring of coal samples at more than 400 coal-fired power plants with generating capacity of 25 MW or more. The data that the plants report on a weekly basis, for a year, will enable EPA to determine whether mercury emissions should be controlled under CAAA. EPA estimated the cost for coal testing at $23,000 per facility. EPA also plans to randomly select 30 power plants for quarterly stack emission tests to determine the quantity and speciation of mercury emitted. Costs for such tests are estimated at $167,000 per facility.

Mercury emission control presents a unique challenge to utilities, because once the chemical is collected, its volatility may result in re-emission. Measurements of mercury emissions from municipal sewage sludge and landfills demonstrates this ability. Mercury speciation by itself influences the risk of re-emission. The elemental form volatizes more readily and defeats the purpose of collecting the mercury in the first place.

Greenhouse gases

The environmental issue overshadowing all others recently has been greenhouse gas emissions. "Global climate change" became a familiar phrase in December 1997, as the Conference of the Parties adopted the Kyoto Protocol to the United Nations Framework Convention on Climate Change that set goals for worldwide CO_2 reductions.

Greenhouse gases—with particular emphasis on CO_2–were addressed in Kyoto. This includes so-called Annex I (developed) countries that accounted for 55% of the Annex 1 CO_2 emissions in 1990. (The U.S. accounted for 34% of Annex 1 CO_2 emissions in 1990.) If ratified, the protocol legally binds Annex 1 countries to reduce aggregate emissions of the greenhouse gases by at least 5% below 1990 levels by 2008-2012. Targeted percentages below 1990 levels for selected countries are as follows: U.S., 7%; European Union, 8%; Japan, 6%; and Russian federation, 0%.

The full U.S. ramifications of the Kyoto Protocol are far from clear and the Congress seems opposed to its ratification. Also, the Edison Electric Institute (EEI) has pointed out that the protocol does not meet the following two standards agreed upon in Senate Resolution 98, passed unanimously in July 1997:

- Any agreement mandating new greenhouse gas limits for developed countries must also mandate commitments for new greenhouse gas limits on developing countries in the same compliance period. As the protocol now stands, the developing countries have no such commitments and the developed countries shoulder most of the burden. While the U.S., Russia, and China produced 40% and consumed 42% of the world's energy in 1996, according to EIA, China—the largest developing nation— is expected to surpass the U.S. as the single largest source of greenhouse gases by 2015. Brazil, India, Indonesia, South Korea, and Mexico major trade competitors to the U.S.—are also excluded from commitments
- Any agreement should not result in serious harm to the U.S. economy. The U.S. will have to reduce its emissions by nearly 30% from projected 2010 levels to reach the proposed 7% reduction. The Clinton administration estimates that to reach a less stringent 1990 level will cost the electric utility industry $30 billion in 2010 and $52 billion in 2020

Studies by Resource Data International, WEFA Inc., and CONSAD Research Corp. all support the contentions raised by EEI: Meeting the terms of the Kyoto Protocol will be impossible without sharp increases in energy costs, loss of jobs, and significant changes in the U.S. standard of living. According to the CONSAD study, the American workforce would decline by approximately 3.1 million workers by the year 2010.

U.S. electric generating plants emitted more than 2.6 billion tons of carbon dioxide in 1996, split about 80-20 between electric utilities and

*Fig. 11-11. Distribution of
Emissions Among Major
Source Categories*

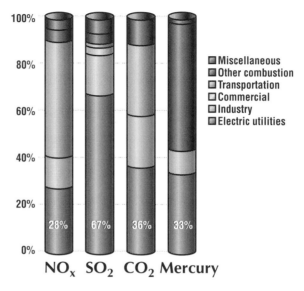

nonutility power producers. The vast majority of generating-unit CO_2 emissions—more than 73%—come from coal-fired power plants, with about 15% from gas-fired facilities, and the rest spread among petroleum plants and other fuel-fired units (Fig. 11-11).

With just 5% of the world's population, the U.S. accounts for 20% of all manmade carbon emissions. As noted above, however, the U.S. share of greenhouse gas emissions will fall substantially in the future as developing countries—notably India and China—bring huge amounts of fossil-fired generating capacity on-line to meet rising demand.

Several methods are available to reduce CO_2 emissions or capture it once formed, including efficiency improvements and CO_2 sequestration. Although power plant efficiencies are rising, through the use of more advanced gas and steam turbines, this efficiency gain cannot offset the projected increase in CO_2 emissions brought about by the construction of more plants to satisfy growing world electricity demand. Capture and disposal of

CO_2, therefore, is being investigated in great detail. Deep ocean, deep aquifers, depleted gas reservoirs, and depleted oil reservoirs are all being examined for their CO_2 storage potential. The technology needed and costs associated with transporting vast quantities of CO_2 to these locations is also under investigation. The Department of Energy is also funding various novel approaches to carbon sequestration that may offer long-term solutions.

According to recent EIA data, significant energy price increases may be required for the U.S. to meet the reductions in greenhouse gas emissions in the Kyoto Protocol. EIA has concluded that the costs of the protocol will depend on the number of permits that can be purchased internationally, on projects to reduce emissions or develop sinks in other countries, and on domestic actions to reduce other gases and develop sinks. These actions may reduce compliance costs by offsetting reductions in energy-related carbon emissions.

Toxics Release Inventory

The Toxics Release Inventory (TRI), a database maintained by EPA, was created to assist emergency response teams that react quickly to accidental releases, and to encourage voluntary emission reductions by industry. The database contains information on specified toxic chemicals released, reduced, and recycled from designated facilities. Coal- and oil-fired generating plants were added to the list in 1997 due to TRI chemicals being created in the production of electricity. Natural gas and nuclear plants were excluded from reporting.

Beginning in 1998, affected power plants had to estimate the release to air, water, or land of each reportable chemical or mixture. Reports will cover individual plants or adjoining multiple plants; ash ponds are included in the affected sites. Facilities that fail to report may incur fines up to $25,000 per day. The utility industry is generally upset with this provision because it will entail additional administrative costs it believed it had succeeded in recent years in convincing EPA that power plant waste streams (particularly ash) were benign and stable.

The utility industry is also regulated by the Clean Water Act (CWA) because it uses large amounts of water. According to EPA, electric utilities account for more than 92% of the total water used for industrial cooling in the U.S. CWA mandates the development of regulations for cooling water intakes for the protection of fish and other aquatic life. Beginning in 1998, all steam-electric generating plants will be required to complete questionnaires providing data that will be reviewed by EPA. Based on the results, some plants will be required to quantitatively assess their adverse impacts on fish populations.

Merchant Plants

12

nheard of a few short years ago, merchant power is now at the forefront of the electric power industry. Merchant plants have been popping up all across the industry landscape recently, and they appear to be the future of a once-stagnant field. Merchant plants are electric power plants built without long-term power purchase contracts. Almost all of the merchant plants are gas-fired and many are being built by gas companies, or by electric companies using them as partners. Many of the merchants are not true merchants, in that they do have contracts for part of their power capacity, just not all of it. Merchant plants that have contracts for part of their production are called anchored merchants.

Merchant plants are currently operating in several countries around the world—countries where electricity markets are sufficiently open to permit competitive, non-binding power generation and sale. The merchant power phenomenon promises to expand in the future, as the global push for utility privatization and rationalized electricity pricing demands the rapid availability of low-cost, highly efficient generating plants.

The merchants offer both opportunities and risks—opportunities to generate extra revenues by taking advantage of market fluctuations in fuel and electricity prices, and risks regarding the plant's ability to recover costs without a sales contract in place. In a relatively short period of time—perhaps a decade or less—the merchant phenomenon will likely be a dying fad in certain countries, as all power plants will represent "merchant" capacity.

Although several countries sport merchant power markets—some quite advanced—nowhere is the explosion more evident than in the U.S. As the U.S. electric utility industry continues to deregulate, independent power producers, unregulated utility subsidiaries, venture capitalists, and power marketers are recognizing the profit possibilities associated with power plants that can more effectively and more quickly react to favorable market conditions.

Merchant plants can be created through various mechanisms. Existing capacity can be converted to merchant capacity. The divestiture of generating assets, primarily in California and the northeast, is freeing significant capacity for merchant operation. On the order of 80 GW of U.S. generating capacity, representing more than 300 plants, has been auctioned or is to be put up for sale. Much of this will be converted into merchant power assets. California's three investor-owned utilities, for example, are selling more than 15 GW of generating capacity as part of that state's deregulation stipulations. Plant repowering is another method for converting existing generation to merchant status. Additional capacity can often be added at much lower cost, and at higher efficiency, than new construction.

A second merchant power mechanism is buyout of existing power purchase agreements from qualifying facilities created through the Public Utility Regulatory Policy Act. Freed from contracts, these facilities will be able to sell merchant power into a region's wholesale market if they're able to generate electricity competitively.

The third, and most exciting merchant power mechanism, is new construction. Though permitting is complicated and expensive, new construction enables plant developers to fashion the plant to the unique energy

Fig. 12–1. Merchant Plant Activity

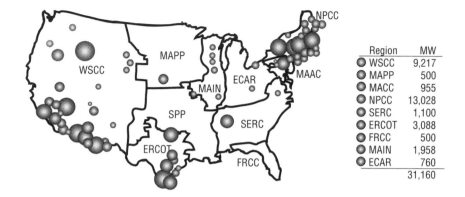

Region	MW
● WSCC	9,217
● MAPP	500
● MACC	955
● NPCC	13,028
● SERC	1,100
● ERCOT	3,088
● FRCC	500
● MAIN	1,958
● ECAR	760
	31,160

demands of a given region, e.g., a neighboring industrial facility may be able to use a portion of the merchant plant's steam and electricity output, while the leftover electricity is sold into the grid.

There is more than 25 GW of merchant capacity currently operational, under construction, under active development, or under consideration in the U.S. Not surprisingly, the bulk of the merchant power experience and interest is in states with historically high electricity prices: California, Massachusetts, Rhode Island, Connecticut and New York. Texas, despite having relatively low electricity prices, is also a merchant hotbed because many of its industrial facilities can take some of the merchant plant's steam and/or electricity output (Fig. 12-1).

Gas domination

The bulk of merchant capacity—both existing, converted facilities, and new construction—is gas-fired, often in a combined-cycle arrangement. Currently, about 90% of the projects under development are fired by natural gas. Because of their lower installed cost, shorter construction times, and efficiencies that are higher than coal-fired and oil-fired units, gas turbine units are the logical choice for merchant capacity. Gas-fired plants also offer significant operational flexibility, being able to provide power cost-effectively in base load, peaking, and load-following capacities. State-of-the-art natural gas combined-cycle plants have total costs, including capital recovery, in the $30-$40/MWh range, with variable costs of $15-$25/MWh. In certain parts of the U.S.—places where existing plant costs can be more than $40/MWh—merchant construction and operation will be economically viable.

New "greenfield" merchant plants benefit significantly from recent advances in gas turbine technology. The world's leading gas turbine manufacturers can now deploy heavy-duty gas turbines that offer combined-cycle efficiencies approaching 60%. Through the U.S. Department of Energy's Advanced Turbine Systems program, the next class of gas turbines will achieve combined-cycle efficiencies greater than 60% by the turn of the century. Their high efficiency reduces fuel requirements, decreases variable fuel costs, and results in fewer emissions per unit of electrical output. This is particularly important in light of potential carbon dioxide emission regulations arising from the Kyoto commitments made in late 1997. As efficiency increases, carbon dioxide emissions decrease correspondingly. Other emissions are further reduced through the application of advanced technology such as low-NO_x burners and catalytic combustion.

Merchant plant projects span the capacity spectrum. Plants as small as 40 MW and plants as large as 1,000 MW are scheduled for merchant operation. The majority of new plant construction, however, is in the 250-400 MW range, a range that maximizes the application of efficient gas turbines and combined cycles (Fig. 12-2).

Despite the preference for gas-fired generation, there are indications that some non-gas generating plants will be converted or built for merchant operation. Much of the divested capacity, for example, consists of coal, oil, and hydroelectric units that may be used as merchant generators.

With all of the new merchant construction under way or planned, there is some concern that too much new capacity could lead to low market prices or unprofitable plants. Resource Data International (RDI) examined the New

Fig. 12–2. Central and South West's 330 MW Sweeny Cogeneration Plant in Texas was the first purpose-built merchant plant to go on line. It entered service late in 1997. It was a 1998 Power Engineering *"Project of the Year" award winner.*

England electricity market with and without merchant capacity. For a hypothetical July 2000 scenario, market prices averaged approximately $9/MWh **higher** without the new merchant capacity than with it. According to the analysis, if all proposed merchant plants were built in the region, the market price probably would be below the $30-$40/MWh threshold needed for new plants to be economic.

International perspective

Merchant power development outside the U.S. is concentrated in those countries where the electric generation industry has been privatized and/or deregulated or is beginning to be. As governments move away from complete control of generation, transmission, and distribution, independent power producers are able to identify and exploit electricity demand opportunities-often by using merchant plants. The United Kingdom, Argentina,

Chile, Columbia, Peru, Norway, Australia and Canada are all exhibiting some signs of merchant power momentum.

In the gas-fired furor that has swept across the United Kingdom (U.K.) since deregulation of its utility industry in the early 1990s, numerous gas-fired combined-cycle power plants have been built or proposed, each of which will have to bid into the U.K. electricity pool on a merchant basis. The late 1997 announcement that no additional gas-fired power plants would be approved for the time being, however, may be an indication of growing pains in the U.K. merchant power industry.

Many other countries are taking steps that would open the door to merchant power plant operation. Privatization of government-owned generation, and liberalized investment policies that promote foreign asset ownership, are two of the more common actions under consideration. The European Union, for example, was scheduled to open 25% of its electricity market to competition by 1999, which should invite merchant power development. Integration of the European Union countries' electricity industries will also increase merchant power's viability.

Risks and finances

A merchant power plant's defining characteristic is its risk exposure. Without a long-term sales agreement for its output, a merchant plant must generate electricity at a cost low enough that the power pool desires its output, while still covering costs, recovering capital, and making a profit. Because of their inherent speculative nature, most merchant financing is through equity investment from cash-rich developers, buoyed by funds from venture capitalists and banks with a high tolerance to risk. Equity investment approaches 50% for merchant plants, compared with less than 20% for conventional, independent power plants.

As the merchant power market matures, more third parties are considering investments, tempted by the prospect of 15 to 20% returns. Various insurance companies, institutional investors, and pension plans have committed funds to planned merchant projects.

For a merchant plant to be successful, effective risk management is essential. The extent of risk mitigation depends on the investors' risk tolerance, but there are mitigation measures for each type of investor. An obvious mitigation tool is market exposure. Rather than positioning the plant as a "pure" merchant—in which none of the plant output is contractually committed—the plant can be established as a hybrid or anchored merchant, in which some of the plant output is committed to the local grid or to a local industrial customer, with the rest free to respond to spot-market opportunities.

Primary risks involved in merchant power development include regulatory and legal risks, fuel market risk, power market risk, plant operating risk, and financing structure risk. To better its chances to receive financing, merchant projects must mitigate these risks. Regulatory risks come from the continuing unfolding of deregulation in the electric power industry. Merchant power facilities are generally sited in areas where regulators have welcomed customer choice and competitive power. It helps reduce risk if deregulation is set on a fairly clear path and if participants understand legislation proposed for the market. Another regulatory risk to merchant power is the unresolved issue of stranded costs. Utilities that own generating plants with high production costs are looking for aid to make their power competitive, but if these utilities do not receive help they could face insolvency. FERC Order 888 requires some mitigation efforts on the part of the utilities, but the primary form of aid will come from wholesale customers who will have to pay fees to change suppliers. Merchant plants that can avoid these transition charges will be better positioned to compete.

The power market presents risks regarding its forecast growth. Merchant providers must assess *total* generation and transmission capacity—how these functions are priced and how the new plant will fit into the market.

Fuel risk is the largest single expense for power generators, and the merchant plant's ability to properly manage both fuel supply and price risk will be very important to the facility's success. Merchant plants without contractual agreements for fuel supply and pricing will be at risk if fuel prices escalate and they're competing against plants with long-term, low-price fuel agreements. They could also be at risk of not receiving adequate amounts of fuel during peak power-pricing times. Fuel contracts are vital for stabilizing fuel risks at merchant plants. Hedging can be used to provide flexibility while protecting the plant from price spikes.

Today's power plants are high-technology driven, and that technology presents both advantage and disadvantage. It is important for plants to operate efficiently and without problems and excessive downtime. A plant using a newly developed gas turbine will need to acquire equipment guarantees of a longer term than the standard one-year manufacturer's guarantee. Other equipment guarantees may also be needed to ensure operating availability.

Developers are concerned with the need to profitably market power and maintain sales volume. Industry leaders predict an increased need for equity investment in merchant facilities—as much as 40 or 50% of the total capital cost. Independent power projects with long-term power purchase agreements typically have only about 20% equity investment.

In October of 1998, Houston Industries, Inc. and Sempra Energy announced the completion of financing for El Dorado Energy, a 492 MW, natural gas-fired power plant in Boulder City, Nevada. This was the first true merchant power plant in the U.S. to be financed with non-recourse debt. The $165 million that was financed represented approximately 60% of the $263 million total project cost.

Other industries

The merchant power concept is not revolutionary. In fact, the power industry's use of guaranteed revenue through long-term contracts to secure financing is more the exception than the rule. "Merchant" type projects are everywhere—toll roads, pulp and paper facilities, sports arenas, entertainment complexes, and petrochemical facilities. All of these projects can and do receive financing. Toll roads, for example, are built with long-term financing without any contractual arrangements regarding the number of vehicles that will pay tolls. Amusement complexes, including fabulous and expensive theme parks, are built with no guarantees regarding the number of paying customers.

These projects all have market risk. No one can guarantee the number of customers that will patronize a private business, or how much the public will pay for a ticket to a sports event.

Distributed Generation

13

d istributed generation is becoming an increasingly popular solution for the future power needs of the U.S., especially in light of the continuing deregulation of electric power. Tying the merchant power trend to distributed generation allows developers to take advantage of these opportunities in which traditional utility plants are not the best solution.

Large utility plants may sometimes be at a disadvantage in a competitive environment. They can generate a large amount of electricity at a moderate price, but running these plants at low loads can be problematic. In addition, transmission infrastructure construction is becoming more and more of an expense and problem for utilities. Distributed generation plants can avoid both problems by enabling capacity to be installed where it is needed. When a small power generation unit is placed on-site, or very close to the facility or facilities that need the power, it can eliminate costly overbuilding of capacity and expensive transmission line construction.

The "mini-merchant" for distributed generation is a new concept. It refers to a distributed generation facility that seeks to match its generating portfolio to a local or regional electricity demand profile in the most efficient and economic way. These plants are typically cogeneration facilities, with overall thermal efficiencies as high as 88%. When compared directly to the separate production of electricity and thermal energy, these plants can reduce CO_2 emission by 50% for the same amount of useful energy. They may also reduce the amount of fuel used by up to 50%.

The success of the mini-merchant plant model hinges on overall economics and how cogeneration and distributed generation fit together. For distributed-generation merchant facilities to work well, several characteristics must exist: flexible dispatch, load following, duty cycle, cogeneration, power production, and defined service territory. These plants can be run on internal combustion engines or gas turbines (Figs. 13-1 and 13-2).

The production capacity must be capable of being dispatched, cycling on and off based on the price of alternative sources of electricity. To facilitate dispatch, the mini-merchant responds to base load, intermediate load, and peak load demand requirements. Effective dispatch requires that all engines be capable of starting and synchronizing in less than 30 seconds. In most cases, this capability will be unnecessary, but could be required. Rapid load changes must be accommodated without tripping off the load and maintenance should not be affected by repeated starting and stopping of the

Fig. 13–1. The Wartsila 1,200-rpm 18V220 SG engine provides intermediate load power. It is rated at 2.5 MW.

Fig. 13–2. Gas Power System's 1.2 MW Innovator genset can use liquid or gaseous fuels

units. These abilities make these small plants far more flexible than standard utility-scale units.

For distributed-generation applications, load-following capabilities are essential. Reciprocating engine efficiency is reasonably flat—between 40% and 100% load for individual generators. Several engines make it possible to load follow a local area from base to peak with little effect on efficiency. Large-scale utility plants do not enjoy this luxury. They generally have limited load range for top efficiency.

The difference between base load and peak averages 100%. For instance, electricity load in the summer months is low at night, when many industrial customers are closed and air conditioners are running very little. During the day, when industrial customers are running and air conditioners are cycling, power demand jumps 100%, or more.

To minimize the capital cost for a distributed-generation plant, it is important to match the generating equipment type to the expected duty. Peaking requirements are met through peaking generating equipment, intermediate generation is used for intermediate needs, and base load equipment provides for base load needs.

Thermal energy production—cogeneration—helps optimize efficiency for distributed generation facilities. Thermal energy production must be reliable (with or without electricity production) for this ability to truly be an asset. Natural gas engines have a fairly high exhaust temperature—of more than 770°F—corresponding to a plant thermal capacity of more than 24 MW. Heat is recovered from exhaust gases and satisfies thermal needs in the facility.

The amount of electricity produced at a cogeneration/distributed-generation plant or mini-merchant is determined by the size of the thermal host. This ensures that production efficiency is maintained at an optimum level. When there is little thermal need, all generation costs are absorbed on the electricity side, with none going to a thermal power cost center. If electricity is needed at a time when thermal needs are low, the decision to produce electricity versus buying it from outside will depend on a comparison of the incremental cost of production and purchase. Normally, the cost of purchasing outside electricity is lowest when weather is moderate. Extremes in climate in both summer and winter increase electrical demands.

In the open market, there are times when low electricity load conditions on the grid, force utilities to discount their energy to near zero pricing. When this happens, on-site generating facilities need to have the flexibility to purchase that low-cost outside power. The goal of distributed generation, however, is to minimize reliance on the transmission grid for peaking and intermediate generation, and to produce base load generation when it is economically practical.

Using distributed generation resources, sited close to loads, allows utilities and other energy service providers to:

- Provide peak shaving in high-load growth areas
- Avoid difficulties in permitting or gaining approval for transmission line rights-of-way
- Reduce transmission line costs and associated electrical losses
- Provide inside-the-fence cogeneration at customers' industrial or commercial sites

Combustion turbines

Two types of combustion turbines are available for 1 MW to 25 MW distributed generation. Heavy-frame models are relatively rugged, with massive casings and rotors. Aeroderivative designs based on aircraft turbofan engines are much lighter than the heavy-frame models and operate at higher temperature ratios. They also have higher compression rations, so aeroderivative units have better simple-cycle efficiencies and lower exhaust gas temperatures than heavy-frame models.

Combustion turbine designs typically have dual-fuel operation capability, with natural gas as the primary fuel and a high quality distillate, such as No. 2 oil, as a back-up fuel. Because gas turbines have relatively high fuel-gas pressure requirements, a natural gas compressor is usually needed unless the plant happens to be sited near a high-pressure cross-country natural gas pipeline. Combustion turbines typically require a minimum natural gas pressure of about 260 psi, while aeroderivative engines require a minimum natural gas pressure as high as 400 psi. A gas compressor can increase total plant cost by 5 to 10%.

Maintenance costs for heavy-frame units can be about one-half that of aeroderivative units. Major maintenance of heavy-frame units may occur on-site, with an outage of about one week for a major overhaul. With aeroderivative units, the gas generator can be replaced with a leased engine, minimizing the power replacement costs associated with the maintenance outage. Aeroderivative engines can be replaced in two or three shifts, and the removed engine can be overhauled off-site.

Reciprocating engines

Reciprocating engines vary greatly in design and in the fuel they burn. Natural gas-fired engines are known as spark ignition or SI engines. Diesel oil-fired engines are known as compression ignition or CI engines. Compression ignition engines can also burn natural gas and a small amount of diesel fuel used as an ignition source. These are known as dual-fuel engines.

Distributed generation facilities using reciprocating engines often have several units, rating from 1 to 15 MW each. Medium-speed and high-speed engines derived from train, marine and truck engines are best suited for distributed generation because of their proven reliability, high efficiency, and low installed cost. High-speed engines are generally favored for standby applications and medium-speed engines are generally best suited for peaking and base load duty.

Reciprocating engines have long been used as energy generators in the U.S. However, overseas their ruggedness and versatility have made them popular choices for remote power needs.

Reciprocating engines have a higher efficiency than combustion turbines, although efficiency falls as unit size decreases. Aeroderivative turbines have higher efficiency than heavy-frame combustion turbines in this small size range.

Reliability and availability are important cost-related issues for distributed generation facilities. A 1993 survey found that 56 medium-speed engines at 18 different plants had an average availability of more than 91%. Combustion turbine plants demonstrate availabilities exceeding 95%.

Environmental performance of these technologies depends on what emission is being considered. For NO_x and CO_2, combustion turbine emissions are 50% to 70% lower than those of reciprocating engines. The NO_x and CO_2 emissions can make it difficult to get permits for reciprocating engines in some states. For CO_2 emissions, reciprocating engines have lower emissions than combustion turbines because of their higher simple-cycle efficiency.

Potential

The worldwide market for distributed-generation-size combustion turbines and reciprocating engines has grown in recent years.

Combustion turbines saw 250 orders in the 1 to 5 MW range in 1997, down from 280 orders in 1996. There were 187 orders in the 5 to 7.5 MW range in 1997, up from 135 orders in 1996. There were 240 orders in the 5 to 15 MW range, up from 49 the previous year.

Reciprocating engines in the 1 to 3.5 MW range saw 4,400 orders in 1997, up from only 1,200 in 1990. There were about 2,100 continuous duty engines sold in 1997, up from 1,300 in 1996. About 370 peaking-duty engines were sold in 1997, down from 870 sold in 1996.

Distributed power systems account for less than 2 GW of electric power, but they are expected to provide as much as 50 GW by 2015.

Fuel cells

Fuel cells are poised to make significant contributions to the growing distributed generation trend. After more than 150 years of research and testing, the basic science has been developed and necessary materials improvements have been made to make fuel cells a commercial reality. Phosphoric acid fuel cells—the technology with the earliest promise for large-scale generation—are now being offered commercially, with more than 100 200 kW units installed worldwide. More advanced designs, such as carbonate fuel cells and solid-oxide fuel cells, are the focus of major electric utility efforts to bring the technology to commercial viability.

Fig. 13–3. A Single Cell from a Fuel Cell

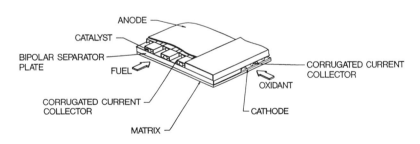

ANODE
CATALYST
BIPOLAR SEPARATOR PLATE
FUEL
CORRUGATED CURRENT COLLECTOR
OXIDANT
CORRUGATED CURRENT COLLECTOR
CATHODE
MATRIX

Fuel cells can best be described as continuously operating batteries or as an electrochemical engine. Like batteries, fuel cells produce power without combustion or rotating machinery. They make electricity by combining hydrogen ions drawn from a hydrogen-containing fuel with oxygen atoms. Batteries provide the fuel and oxidant internally, which is why they must be recharged periodically. Fuel cells, on the other hand, take these key ingredients from outside the system and continuously produce power for as long as the fuel and oxidant supplies are maintained (Fig. 13–3).

Fuel cells use these ingredients to create chemical reactions that produce either hydrogen- or oxygen-bearing ions at one of the cell's two electrodes. These ions pass through an electrolyte such as phosphoric acid or carbonate (which conducts electricity), and react with oxygen atoms. The result is an electric current at both electrodes, with waste heat and water vapor as exhaust products. The current is proportional to the size of the electrodes. The voltage is limited electrochemically to about 1.23 volts per electrode pair, or cells. Cells can be stacked until the desired power level is reached. Several stacks can be combined into a "module" for site installation. The waste heat from fuel cells is well-suited for cogeneration or process heat applications.

Fuel cells offer great potential in the distributed generation field for several reasons. Because they are installed in small modules, an industrial customer or utility can install the amount of power needed, eliminating extra up-front costs for power that will not be needed for several years. When more power is needed, more fuel cell modules can be added quickly and easily, with low overhead. The cogeneration and process heat functions of fuel cells are of great appeal to industrial customers, which are currently the great majority of distributed generation providers. Fuel cells also offer very short lead times from order placement to installed power generation capacity.

Fuel cell costs have been falling rapidly in recent years, and they should soon become economically competitive with other technologies, especially where strict environmental compliance is required. Operating costs are competitive as well, particularly if operators consider the fuel cell plant's high efficiency and reliability when operating at partial loads. Siting and operating flexibilities can translate into site-specific dollar savings.

Growth trends

The U.S. industrial sector accounts for about one-fourth of the nation's total energy use. Its distributed generation load is expected to increase its demand for energy by 1.3% annually over the next couple of decades, resulting in a more than 25% jump in that sector's demand by 2018.

The Gas Research Institute projects that total industrial energy consumption will grow from 27.3 quadrillion Btu (quads) in 1995 to 35.1 quads in 2015. During that same period, industrial consumption of natural gas will increase from 10 quads in 1995 to 13 quads in 2015. Natural gas has a dominant share of industry's competitive fuel and power segment—about 40%—and this share is expected to be maintained during the projection period. The market includes boilers, industrial cogeneration, and process heat.

In the competitive fuel and power markets, natural gas is expected to increase its share of the boiler market at the expense of coal; grow in the cogeneration markets as a reflection of end user preference for natural gas, combined-cycle technologies; and maintain its dominant share of the process heat sector.

Conclusion

14

t he combination of increased efficiencies in the natural gas delivery system and wellhead price deregulation has led to generally declining prices for consumers. There is hope that much the same may be true of electricity deregulation, once that process gets a bit further along. But as prices fall and margins narrow, companies need all available tools to ensure profitability in a competitive marketplace. Synergies of business and the opportunities awaiting in a deregulated environment are driving the current convergence between the two industries. More and more, these industries are overlapping and blending together. The purpose of this book has been to help readers understand both these vibrant industries and the links that tie one to the other.

According to a study by the American Gas Association, retail prices for natural gas for all consuming sectors were on average 18% lower in 1996 than in 1987, when the effects of wellhead price deregulation began to appear. The declines by sectors were: residential 14%, commercial 25%, industrial 19%, and electric generation 12%. (All numbers are adjusted for inflation.) Deregulation proponents anticipate similar results from deregulation of electricity, although it is too soon to tell whether their predictions are accurate.

Data from the Department of Energy shows natural gas to be the "best energy value". The DOE data showed that in 1998 natural gas cost $6.19 per million Btu, compared with $24.68 for electricity and $6.85 for heating oil. The costs per Btu are equivalent to 61.9 cents per therm for natural gas, 8.42 cents per kilowatt-hour for electricity, and 95 cents per gallon for heating oil. (These DOE figures are used in cost estimates for the Federal Trade Commission appliance labeling program, designed to help consumers choose equipment that is the most economical to operate.) Propane came in a $10.39 per million Btu or 95 cents per gallon, while kerosene was $7.48 per million Btu or $1.01 a gallon.

Natural gas is abundantly available through domestic resources, with the great majority of the natural gas imports coming from Canada and Mexico. This makes the fuel economical and reliable. Global events are unlikely to adversely affect supply. Gas supply in the U.S. continues to exceed consumption. The latest data from the Energy Information Administration shows reserve additions have exceeded production for the past several years. New discoveries continue to be made, and replacement of reserves is running at about 105%, making the gas supply more and more secure.

This security adds to the appeal of natural gas as fuel for electric power. Other factors in its favor include low emissions, ease of transport and storage, and high efficiency technology.

Although prices are affected by weather patterns and seasonal demand, natural gas consumption is steadily growing, with a good part of that growth coming through utility additions and retrofits. Natural gas use in 1998 was expected to exceed 23 quads, the highest level of gas consumption ever achieved, breaking the record set in 1972. Gas consumption has jumped 35% in the past decade, which is phenomenal for an industry as mature as natural gas.

As demand for electricity continues to grow, and demand for natural gas-fired generation grows with it, these two industries will continue their stream of mergers, acquisitions, partnerships, and alliances—building the Btu industry of tomorrow.

Appendix A
Convergence/Btu Glossary

A

Acid rain Rain with a pH below 5.6. Rain normally has a pH of around 5.6, which is slightly acidic. Rain becomes more acidic when nitric and sulfuric acids from nitrogen oxides and sulfur oxides are released into the atmosphere. One of the most common ways these oxides are released is through the burning of fossil fuels.

Actuator A controlled motor that converts electricity to action, or any device that converts voltage or current into a mechanical output.

Adiabatic Any change in which there is no gain or loss of heat.

Affiliated power producer A company that generates power and is affiliated with a utility.

Aggregation The process of estimating demand and scheduling deliveries of power to a group of customers.

Aggregator A company that consolidates a number of individual users and/or supplies into a group. Marketing companies that pool gas from many sources into packages for resale to local distribution companies or end users.

Air monitoring   Intermittent or continuous testing of emission air for pollution levels.

Air pollution   Contaminants in the atmosphere that have toxic characteristics and which are believed to be harmful to the health of animal or plant life.

Air quality   Air quality is determined by the amount of pollutants and contaminants present.

Alkaline   A substance with a pH greater than seven.

All-events contracts   Also called "hell or high-water contracts". Sales or transport contracts requiring the customer to take or pay for contracted volumes or services, even if the seller is unable to deliver, regardless of who is at fault for the failure.

Allowable emissions   The emissions rate of a stationary source calculated using the maximum rated capacity of the source and the most stringent applicable governmental standards.

Alternating current (ac)   A periodic current, the average value of which over a period is zero. Unless distinctly specified otherwise, the term refers to a current that reverses its direction at regularly recurring intervals of time and that has alternately positive and negative values. Almost all electric utilities generate ac electricity because it can easily be transformed to higher or lower voltages.

Ambient conditions   The outside weather conditions, including temperature, humidity, and barometric pressure. Ambient conditions can affect the available capacity of a power plant.

American Wire Gauge (AWG)   The standard wire size measuring system in the U.S. Abbreviated AWG.

Ammeter   A device used to measure an electric current's magnitude, by amperes, milliamperes, microamperes, or kiloamperes.

Ampere   A unit of measurement of electric current produced in a circuit by one volt acting through a resistance of one ohm.

Ancillary services   Services necessary to support the transmission of energy from resources to loads while maintaining reliable operation of the transmission provider's transmission system. Examples include voltage control and spinning dispatch.

Anticline A geologic feature in which the constituent rock strata have been compressed laterally into an inverted U-shaped fold. Anticlines are frequently traps for oil and gas. Structural counterparts of anticlines are synclines, which are concave folds as viewed from above.

APPA American Public Power Association. The trade association of publicly held power entities.

Arc A discharge of electricity through a gas or air.

Arms-length transactions Transactions between unaffiliated companies. i.e., sales by a gas producer to an unrelated local distribution company.

Associated gas Natural gas found in association with crude oil, either as "dissolved" or "solution" gas within the oil-bearing strata or as "gas cap" gas just above the oil zone.

Attainment area A geographic area under the Clean Air Act which is in compliance with the Act's national Ambient Air Quality Standards. This designation is made on a pollution-specific basis.

Availability The unit of measure for the actual time a transmission line or generating unit is capable of providing service, if needed.

Available but not needed capability Net capability of main generating units that are operable but not considered necessary to carry load, and cannot be connected to load within 30 minutes.

Average revenue per kilowatt-hour The average revenue per kilowatt-hour of electricity sold by sector (residential, commercial, industrial, or other) and geographic area (State, Census division, and national), is calculated by dividing the total monthly revenue by the corresponding total monthly sales for each sector and geographic area.

Avoided cost A utility company's production or transmission cost avoided by conservation or purchasing from another source rather than by building a new generation facility.

B

Back-stopping   Arranging for alternate supplies of gas in the event a user's primary source fails to be delivered.

Back-up power   Power supplied to a customer when its normal supply is interrupted.

Barrel   A volumetric unit of measure for crude oil and petroleum products equivalent to 42 U.S. gallons.

Base load   The minimum amount of electric power or natural gas delivered or required over a given period of time at a steady rate. The lowest load level during a utility's daily or annual cycle.

Base load capacity   The generating equipment normally operated to serve loads on an around-the-clock basis.

Base load plant   A plant, usually housing high-efficiency steam-electric units, which is normally operated to take all or part of the minimum load of a system, and which consequently produces electricity at an essentially constant rate and runs continuously. These units are operated to maximize system mechanical and thermal efficiency and minimize system operating costs.

Basins, sedimentary   Geological "provinces" underlain by sediments deemed to be potential source rocks or traps for oil or gas.

Basis   A geographic price differential between a particular market and the delivery point specified in an exchange-traded commodity contract.

Bcf   Billion cubic feet.

Bid week   A period in the latter part of each calendar month during which spot contracts are negotiated for gas to be delivered in the following calendar month.

Biomass   Any body or accumulation of organic material. In the gas industry, biomass refers to the organic waste products of agricultural processing, feedlots, timber operations, or urban refuse from which methane can be derived.

Biotic theory   A theory of hydrocarbon genesis that attributed the origins of the earth's endowment of natural gas and other hydrocarbons exclusively to biological processes. Methane is believed to be the product of organic decomposition of tissues of once-living plants and animals.

Bitumen   Heavy, tar-like hydrocarbons that are nearly solid under atmospheric conditions, and must be heated or blended with lighter hydrocarbons for transmission by pipeline.

Boiler   A device for generating steam for power, processing, or heating purposes or for producing hot water for heating purposes or hot water supply. Heat from an external combustion source is transmitted to a fluid contained within the tubes in the boiler shell. This fluid is delivered to an end user at a desired pressure, temperature, and quality.

Border price   The price of gas at the U.S.-Canadian border, for the purpose of export/import licensing, taxation, or passthrough of costs in downstream sales.

BPA Bonneville Power Administration   A power marketing and electric transmission agency of the U.S. government with headquarters in Portland, Oregon.

Breaker   A device to break the current of a given electric circuit by opening the circuit.

Btu   British thermal unit. A standard unit for measuring the quantity of heat energy equal to the quantity of heat required to raise the temperature of a pound of water by 1°F.

Bulk power   The generation and high-voltage transmission of electricity.

Bundling   1) For electricity, combining the costs of generation, transmission, and distribution and other services into a single rate charged to the retail customer. 2) For natural gas, providing a combination of products and services in a single package at a fixed price with no customer ability to accept less than the entire package.

Burnertip   The ultimate point where natural gas is used by the customer. The burnertip refers to any gas-fueled equipment, such as a furnace, cook top, or engine, used by the customer.

Bus   A conductor or solid bar aluminum or copper used to connect a circuit or circuits to a common interface. For example, the bus bars or conductors in a substation used to connect the low-voltage windings of transformers to the outgoing distribution circuits.

Bushing   An insulating structure including a through conductor with provision for mounting on electrical equipment for the purpose of insulating the conductor from its mounting and conducting current through the mounting.

Butane   A hydrocarbon component of produced natural gas and crude oil. One of the natural gas liquids and a component of liquefied petroleum gas.

Bypass   Direct sales by producers, pipelines, or marketers to end users, avoiding markups or transport fees of incumbent local distribution companies.

C

Cable   A conductor with insulation or a stranded conductor with or without insulation and other coverings or a combination of conductors insulated from one another.

Candela   The standard unit of luminous intensity. One candela is equal to one lumen per steradian.

Cap   Non-permeable rock found above oil and gas reservoirs, which through geologic time prevented these hydrocarbons from dissipating. May also refer to a gas cap on top of a pool of oil.

Capability   The maximum load that a generating unit, generating station, or other electrical apparatus can carry under specified conditions for a given period of time without exceeding approved limits of temperature and stress.

Capacitance   The property of a system of conductors and dielectrics that permits the storage of electricity when potential differences exist between the conductors.

Capacitor bank   An assembly of capacitors and all necessary accessories, such as switching equipment, protective equipment, controls, and other devices needed for a complete operating installation.

Capacity charge An element in a two-part pricing method used in capacity transactions (energy charge is the other element). The capacity charge, sometimes called Demand Charge, is assessed on the amount of capacity being purchased.

Capacity The amount of electric power delivered or required for which a generator turbine, transformer, transmission circuit, station, or system is rated by the manufacturer.

Carbon dioxide A colorless, odorless, nonpoisonous gas which occurs in ambient air. It is produced by fossil fuel combustion or the decay of materials.

Carbon monoxide A colorless, odorless, tasteless, but poisonous gas produced mainly from the incomplete combustion of fossil fuels.

Casinghead gas Natural gas that flows from an oil well along with the liquid petroleum. It is also called associated gas or solution gas because it resides beneath the earth's surface in conjunction with crude oil.

Chlorofluorocarbons A family of inert, nontoxic, easily liquefied chemicals used in refrigeration, air conditioning, packaging, and insulation, or as solvents or aerosol propellants. They are thought to be major contributors to potential ozone thinning and global warming and are therefore becoming increasingly regulated and their use more restricted.

Circuit breaker A device designed to open and close a circuit. It is designed to open automatically on a predetermined overload of current, without injury to itself, when properly applied within its rating.

Circuit recloser A line protection device that interrupts momentary line faults in a distribution system. A circuit recloser will automatically close after a short time and will immediately reopen the circuit if there are still problems.

Circuit A circuit is a conductor or system of conductors forming a closed path through which electric current flows.

City gate The physical interconnection of an interstate natural gas pipeline and the distribution system of a local gas utility. "Behind the city gate" refers to delivery points within the distribution system of the local gas utility.

Cogeneration   The simultaneous production of power and thermal energy, such as burning natural gas to produce electricity and using the heat produced to create steam for industrial use.

Coincidental demand   The sum of two or more demands that occur in the same time interval.

Coincidental peak load   The sum of two or more peak loads that occur in the same time interval.

Coke   The solid carbonaceous residue produced from the destructive distillation of coal or oil. It is a vital material for steel making.

Combination pricing   A pricing strategy in which aspects of cost, demand, and competition pricing methods are integrated.

Combined-cycle unit   An electric generating unit that consists of one or more combustion turbines and one or more boilers with a portion of the required energy input to the boiler(s) provided by the exhaust gas of the combustion turbine(s).

Combined-cycle   An electric generating technology in which additional electricity is produced from otherwise lost waste heat exiting from the gas turbines. The exiting heat is routed to a conventional boiler or to a heat recovery steam generator for utilization by a steam turbine in the production of electricity. The process increases the efficiency of the electricity generating unit.

Combined utility   A public utility, either privately owned or municipally, which sells both gas and electricity.

Combustion air   Air needed to ensure complete fuel combustion.

Combustion chamber   The area where fuel is burned.

Combustion   The rapid chemical combination of a substance with oxygen, usually accompanied by the liberation of heat and light.

Commercial customers   A statistical and regulatory category of energy use, embracing retail and wholesale trade, service establishments, hotels, offices, public institutions, and sometimes apartments that are separately metered.

Commercial operation   Commercial operation begins when control of the loading of the generator is turned over to the system dispatcher. The amount of fuel used for gross generation, providing standby service, start-up and/or flame stabilization.

Commodities   Goods purchased frequently and in large quantities.

Commodity charge   A customer charge for utility service that is proportional to the amount of gas or electricity actually purchased.

Common carrier   A transporter obligated by law to provide service to all interested parties without discrimination to the limit of its capacity. If the capacity of a common-carrier pipeline is insufficient to satisfy demand, it must offer services "ratably" to all shippers in proportion to the amounts they tender for shipment.

Common purchaser   An oil or gas carrier that is required by law to purchase without discrimination from all parties tendering oil or gas produced from a given reservoir, field, or area.

Competitive environment   Rivalry among firms offering similar products or services to the same market.

Compressed natural gas (CNG)   Natural gas that is highly compressed, though not to the point of liquefaction, so that it can be used by an operation not attached to a fixed pipeline. CNG is used as a transport fuel.

Condensate   Light hydrocarbon molecules that are liquid under atmospheric temperatures and pressures, and which are typically extracted from raw natural gas during processing.

Condenser   Condensers are equipment in generating facilities that capture steam and turn it back into water for reuse in the feedwater system of the plant.

Conductor   A material, usually in the form of a wire, cable, or bus bar, suitable for carrying an electric current.

Conduit   A structure designed to hold electric conductors. It could be a metal pipe or other material.

Consumption   The amounts of fuel used for gross generation, providing standby service, start-up, and/or flame stabilization. May also be used to refer to customer use.

Contract carrier   A transporter, such as a gas pipeline company, that provides its service on a discretionary, contractual basis for other parties.

Contract price   Price of fuels marketed on a contract basis covering a period of one or more years. Contract prices reflect market conditions at the time the contract was negotiated and therefore remain constant throughout the life of the contract or are adjusted through escalation clauses. Generally, contract prices do not fluctuate widely.

Contract receipts   Purchases based on a negotiated agreement that generally covers a period of one or more years.

Conventional gas   Gas that can be produced under current technologies at a cost that is no higher than its current market value.

Convergence   The coming together and merging of previously distinct industries. This phenomenon is currently under way for the electricity and fuels industries, particularly electricity and natural gas.

Cooling tower   The portion of a power facility's water circulating system which extracts the heat from water coming out of the plant's condenser, cooling it down and transferring the heat into the air while the water returns through the system to become boiler make-up water.

Cooperative electric utility   An electric utility legally established to be owned by and operated for the benefit of those using its service. The utility company will generate, transmit, and/or distribute supplies of electric energy to a specified area not being serviced by another utility. Such ventures are generally exempt from federal income tax laws. Most electric cooperatives have been initially financed by the Rural Electrification Administration, U.S. Department of Agriculture.

Cost-of-service   The paradigm of gas utility regulation in North America, whereby customer charges are based on the actual or forecast costs of providing the service, rather than allowing prices to rise to whatever customers may be willing to pay.

Covenants   Provisions of debt instruments that limit actions of the borrower that might increase risk of non-performance.

Crude oil   Naturally occurring mixtures of hydrocarbons that are liquid under atmospheric conditions, as opposed to natural gas and bitumens, which are gaseous and solid, respectively, under these conditions. All three phases are often present, and in solution together, within hydro-carbon reservoirs.

Cryogenic   Supercooled. Liquefied natural gas is cryogenically cooled for transport.

Cubic foot   The most common unit of measurement of gas volume; it is the amount of gas required to fill a volume of one cubic foot under stated conditions of temperature, pressure, and water vapor.

Current   The flow of electrons in an electrical conductor. The rate of movement of the electricity, measured in amperes.

Customer density   Number of customers in a given unit of area or on a given length of distribution line.

D

Declining block rates   A utility rate structure by which customers who consume greater quantities are charged lower per-unit rates, which descend in a step-like fashion.

Dedication   Legal reservation of reserves or production from a given property to a specific purpose or customer.

Deep gas   Natural gas located 15,000 feet or more below the earth's surface.

Deliverability   The amount of gas that a pipeline or producer is capable of delivering, as limited by the terms of its supply contracts, its physical plant capacity, or by government regulations.

Demand   Ability and willingness of customers to purchase a product or service. In electricity, the rate at which electric energy is delivered to or by a system, part of a system, or piece of equipment, at a given instant or averaged over any designated period of time.

Demand charge   A customer charge for utility service that reflects the extent to which a particular customer chooses to purchase a right to draw a certain volume of gas at any time during the year.

Demand-side management (DSM)   The term for all activities or programs undertaken by an electric system or its customers to influence the amount and timing of electricity use. Included in DSM are the planning, implementation, and monitoring of utility activities that are designed to influence consumers use of electricity in ways that will produce desired changes in a utility's load shape. These programs are dwindling, and expected to experience a great decline under deregulation.

Department of Energy (DOE)   Established in 1977, the DOE manages programs of research, development and commercialization for various energy technologies, and associated environmental, regulatory, and defense programs. DOE promulgates energy policies and acts as a principal adviser to the President on energy matters.

Deregulation   Relaxing or eliminating laws and regulations controlling an industry or industries.

Direct current (dc)   An electric current that flows in one direction with a magnitude that does not vary or that varies only slightly.

Derivatives   Financial instruments whose values depend on those of other underlying assets. Examples include futures contracts, options, and swaps.

Direct purchases   Purchases of gas by local distribution companies or end users, directly from producers rather than from merchant pipelines.

Disaggregation   The breaking up of the traditional electric utility structure from a totally bundled service to an ala carte service.

Disco   The term for a utility company that has vertically disaggregated and operates its retail distribution business separately from any other power businesses it may own.

Dissolved gas   A form of associated gas found in solution with petroleum and, therefore, produced from oil wells as casinghead gas.

Distribution automation   A system consisting of line equipment, communications infrastructure, and information technology that is used to gather intelligence about the distribution system and provide analysis and control in order to maximize operating efficiency and reliability. It includes small distribution substations, sub-transmission and distribution feeder reclosers, regulators, and sectionalizers, which can be remotely monitored and controlled.

Distribution company   An electric distribution company that provides only distribution services that are unbundled. Abbreviated disco.

Distribution system   1) For natural gas, the pipes and service equipment that carry or control the supply of natural gas from the point of local supply, or city gate, to the customer's meter. 2) For electricity, the substations, transformers, and lines that convey electricity from the generation site to the consumer.

Diversification   When a company becomes involved in products or services aimed at new markets.

Draft   The movement of air into and through a combustion chamber, breeching, stack, and chimney. It can be natural, allowing hot air to rise, or artificial, produced by equipment such as fans.

E

Edison Electric Institute (EEI)   The association of the investor-owned electric utilities in the U.S. and industry affiliates worldwide. Its U.S. members serve almost all of the customers served by the investor-owned segment of the electric utility industry. They generate almost 80% of all electricity generated by utilities and service more than 75% of all customers in the nation. EEI's basic objective is the "advancement in the public service of the art of producing, transmitting, and distributing electricity and the promotion of scientific research in such field". EEI compiles data and statistics relating to the industry and makes them available to member companies, the public, and government representatives.

Electric and magnetic fields (EMF)   Electric and magnetic fields are created when energy flows through an energized conductor. The electric field is from the voltage impressed on the conductors and the magnetic field is from the current in the conductors. These fields surround the conductors. Electric fields are measured in volts per meter or kilovolts per meter and magnetic fields are measured in gauss or tesla. Electric and magnetic fields occur naturally, but can also be created. There is debate regarding possible health effects of these fields when they occur in proximity to residences.

Electric capacity   The ability of a power plant to produce a given output of electric energy at an instant in time. Capacity is measured in kilowatts or megawatts.

Electric current   A flow of electrons in an electrical conductor. The strength or rate of movement of the electricity is measured in amperes.

Electric plant   A facility containing prime movers, electric generators, and auxiliary equipment for converting other types of energy into electric energy.

Electric rate schedule   A statement of the electric rate and the terms and conditions governing its application, including attendant contract terms and conditions that have been accepted by a regulatory body with appropriate oversight authority.

Electric utility   A corporation, person, agency, authority, or other legal entity or instrumentality that owns and/or operates facilities within the U.S., its territories, or Puerto Rico for the generation, transmission, distribution, or sale of electric energy primarily for use by the public and files forms listed in the Code of Federal Regulations, Title 18, Part 141. Facilities that qualify as cogenerators or small power producers under the Public Utility Regulatory Policies Act (PURPA) are not considered electric utilities.

Electricity   The flow of electrons in a conducting material. The flow is called a current.

Emissions   Any waste products leaving a power plant. This term generally applies to air pollution, but it can also apply to soil or water waste issues. There are many substances that can be emitted from power plants, and most of them are regulated and monitored.

End user   The ultimate consumer, as opposed to a customer purchasing for resale.

Energy charge The portion of the charge for electric services that is based on the electric energy either consumed or billed.

Energy deliveries Energy generated by one electric utility system and delivered to another system through one or more transmission lines.

Energy efficiency Refers to programs that are aimed at reducing the energy used by specific end-use devices and systems, typically without affecting the services provided. These programs reduce overall electricity consumption (reported in megawatt-hours), often without explicit consideration for the timing of program-induced savings. Such savings are generally achieved by substituting technically more advanced equipment to produce the same level of end-use services (e.g. lighting, heating, motor drive) with less electricity. Examples include high-efficiency appliances, efficient lighting programs, high-efficiency heating, ventilating and air conditioning (HVAC) systems or control modifications, efficient building design, advanced electric motor drives, and heat recovery systems.

Energy marketer An entity, regulated by the Federal Energy Regulatory Commission (FERC), which arranges bulk power transactions for end users. The main goal of energy marketers is determining the best overall fuel choice for customers, whether it be natural gas, electricity, oil, etc., and then delivering that fuel to the customer. They deal in the open market, taking full title to the energy until they resell it to an end user.

Energy Policy Act of 1992 Legislation which authorized FERC to introduce competition at the wholesale level through new open access requirements for transmission and authorizing exempt wholesale generators.

Energy receipts Energy generated by one electric utility system and received by another system through one or more transmission lines.

Energy source The primary source that provides the power that is converted to electricity through chemical, mechanical, or other means. Energy sources include coal, petroleum and petroleum products, gas, water, uranium, wind, sunlight, geothermal, and other sources.

Energy Power is the capability of doing work. Energy is power supplied over time, expressed in kilowatt-hours. Energy can take on different forms, some of which are easily convertible and can be changed to another form useful for work. Most of the world's convertible energy comes from fossil fuels that are burned to produce heat that is then used as a transfer medium to medium to mechanical or other means in order to accomplish tasks. Electrical energy is usually measured in kilowatt-hours, while heat energy is generally measured in British thermal units.

Enhanced recovery A family of technologies applied to extract more of the hydrocarbons in place in a reservoir than can be produced by natural fluid pressure.

Environmental Protection Agency (EPA) This agency administers federal environmental policies, enforces environmental laws and regulations, performs research, and provides information on environmental subjects.

Ethane A hydrocarbon component of produced natural gas and to a lesser extent of pipeline gas. It is the lightest of the natural gas liquids.

Exempt wholesale generator A company that generates power solely for wholesale use and does not sell it to the public. They are exempt from PUHCA.

Exploration The search for naturally occurring hydrocarbons, including surface studies, seismic and other geophysical surveys, and the drilling of exploratory wells.

Extensions Additions to proved reserves corresponding to increases in the area or volume of known reservoirs. Largely a result of step-out and infill drilling.

Externalities Factors affecting human welfare not included in the monetary cost of a product, such as air pollution caused by power generation.

Extra high voltage (EHV) A term applied to voltage levels of electric power system transmission lines that are higher than 230,000 volts (230 kV).

F

Facility An existing or planned location or site at which prime movers, electric generators, and/or equipment for converting mechanical, chemical, and/or nuclear energy into electric energy are situated, or will be situated. A facility may contain more than one generator of either the same or different prime mover type. For a cogenerator, the facility includes the industrial or commercial process.

Fahrenheit   The temperature scale commonly used in the U.S., with the freezing point of water at 32° and the boiling point at 212° at sea level.

Fault   A partial or total local failure in the insulation or continuity of a conductor in a wire or cable.

Federal electric utilities   A classification of utilities that applies to those that are agencies of the federal government involved in the generation and/or transmission of electricity. Most of the electricity generated by federal electric utilities is sold at wholesale prices to local government-owned and cooperatively owned utilities, and to investor-owned utilities. These government agencies are the Army Corps of Engineers and the Bureau of Reclamation, which generate electricity at federally owned hydroelectric projects. The Tennessee Valley Authority produces and transmits electricity in the Tennessee Valley region.

Federal Energy Regulatory Commission (FERC)   A quasi-independent regulatory agency within the Department of Energy having jurisdiction over interstate electricity sales, wholesale electric rates, hydroelectric licensing, natural gas pricing, oil pipeline rates, and gas pipeline certification.

Federal Power Act   Enacted in 1920, and amended in 1935, the Act consists of three parts. The first part incorporated the Federal Water Power Act administered by the former Federal Power Commission, whose activities were confined almost entirely to licensing non-Federal hydroelectric projects. Parts II and III were added with the passage of the Public Utility Act. These parts extended the Act's jurisdiction to include regulating the interstate transmission of electrical energy and rates for its sale as wholesale in interstate commerce. The Federal Energy Regulatory Commission is now charged with the administration of this law.

Federal Power Commission (FPC)   The predecessor agency of the Federal Energy Regulatory Commission. The FPC was created by an Act of

Congress under the Federal Water Power Act on June 10, 1920. It was charged originally with regulating the electric power and natural gas industries. The FPC was abolished on September 20, 1977, when the Department of Energy was created. The functions of the FPC were divided between the Department of Energy and the Federal Energy Regulauory Commission.

Feeder cable   A cable which extends from a central site along a primary route or from a primary route to a secondary route, thus providing connections to one or more distribution cables.

Feedwater   The water used in the boiler system of generating plants. It is treated to make it as pure as economically feasible to keep the boiler clean and operating properly.

Firm gas   Gas sold on a continuous and generally long-term contract.

Firm power   Power or power-producing capacity intended to be available at all times during the period covered by a guaranteed commitment to deliver, even under adverse conditions.

Firm service   Sales and/or transportation service provided without interruption throughout the year. Firm services are generally provided under filed rate tariffs.

Fixed cost   An expense that does not change in response to varied production levels. Also called imbedded cost.

Flue gas desulfurization unit   Also called a scrubber. Equipment used to remove sulfur oxides from the combustion gases of a boiler plant before discharge into the atmosphere. Chemicals are used to pull oxides from the gases.

Flue gas particulate collectors   Equipment used to remove fly ash from the combustion gases of a boiler plant before discharge into the atmosphere. Particulate collectors include electrostatic precipitators, mechanical collectors, fabric filters or baghouses, and wet scrubbers.

Force majeure   A contractual provision by which a party's obligations are waived if a superior force, such as weather, war or an act of God, makes it impossible for those obligations to be met.

Forward contract A contract for future delivery at a price determined in advance.

Forced outage The shutdown of a generating unit, transmission line or other facility, for emergency reasons or a condition in which the generating equipment is unavailable for load due to unanticipated breakdown.

Fossil fuel plant An electricity producing generating plant that uses coal, petroleum, and/or natural gas as its energy source.

Fossil fuel Any naturally occurring organic fuel, including petroleum, coal, and natural gas.

Franchise A special privilege conferred by a government on an individual or a corporation to engage in a specified line of business, or to use public ways and streets.

Fuel cell A device capable of converting natural gas, hydrogen, or other gaseous fuels directly into electricity and heat via an electrochemical process that avoids the energy losses associated with combustion and the spinning or reciprocation of mechanical parts.

Fuel expenses Costs include the fuel used in the production of steam and/or electricity at an electric power plant. Other associated costs include unloading the shipped fuel and all handling of the fuel up to the point where it enters the power plant. Fuel expenses are generally the largest expense category for electric power generating facilities.

Fuse A device that protects a circuit by fusing open its current-responsive element when an overcurrent or short-circuit current passes through it.

Futures A derivative financial instrument that creates a contractual obligation to buy or sell a specified volume of an underlying commodity at a set price on some future date.

G

Gas cap Gas-rich strata overlying the oil-bearing strata of a petroleum reservoir. A gas cap forms when the ratio of gas to oil in a particular reservoir is too high for all of the gas to remain in solution with the oil.

Gas marketer/broker A non-regulated, competitive buyer/seller of natural gas. The marketer/broker may be an aggregator.

Gas processing Processing raw gas to remove liquid hydrocarbons such as propane and butane, toxic or corrosive substances such as hydrogen sulfide and carbon dioxide, and adjust the residue gas to a standard heating value.

Gas turbine Consists of an axial-flow air compressor and one or more combustion chambers where liquid or gaseous fuel is burned The hot gases that are produced are passed to the turbine where the gases expand to drive the generator and are then used to run the compressor.

Gas A fuel burned under boilers and by internal combustion engines for electric generation. These include natural, manufactured, and waste gas.

Generating unit Any combination of generators, reactors, boilers, combustion turbines, or other prime movers operated together or physically connected to produce electric power.

Generation The process of producing electric energy by transforming other forms of energy. It also refers to the amount of electric energy produced, generally expressed in kilowatt-hours or megawatt-hours.

Generator nameplate capacity The full-load continuous rating of a generator, prime mover, or other electric power production equipment under specific conditions as designated by the manufacturer. Installed generator nameplate rating is usually indicated on a plate physically attached to the generator.

Generator A machine that converts mechanical energy into electrical energy.

Gigawatt (GW) A unit of electric power equal to one billion watts or one thousand megawatts.

Gigawatt-hour (GWh) One billion watt-hours.

Global warming A hypothesized increase in worldwide atmospheric temperatures, caused by an intensification of the natural greenhouse effect thought to attend the socially accelerated accumulation of carbon dioxide and other heat-retaining gases.

Green marketing Using an ecological perspective in marketing, packaging, or promoting a product as environmentally benign or beneficial.

Greenfield plant Refers to a new electric power generating facility built from the ground up on a site that has not been used for industrial uses previously. Essentially a plant that starts with a green field. Plants that are built on sites that have already been used for another power plant or other industrial use are called brownfield plants.

Greenhouse effect   The natural warming of the earth's lower atmosphere, associated with solar energy reflected from the surface and retained by water vapor and irradiative gases, including carbon dioxide and methane.

Greenhouse gases   Those gases, such as carbon dioxide, nitrous oxide, and methane, that are transparent to solar radiation but opaque to longwave radiation. Their action in the atmosphere is similar to that of glass in a greenhouse.

Grid   The layout of an electrical distribution system.

Gross generation   The total amount of electric energy produced by the generating units at a generating station or stations, measured at the generator terminals.

Ground   A conducting connection, whether intentional or accidental, by which an electric circuit or equipment is connected to the earth, to some conducting body of relatively large extent that serves in place of the earth.

H

Heat rate   A power plant term for the efficiency of the power plant. Heat rate measures how much of the fuel that is burned actually turns into electricity. Heat rate is generally represented as a mixture of British and metric units, Btu/kWh.

Heating value   The amount of heat produced by the complete combustion of a unit quantity of fuel. Heating value for gas is specified as either "gross" or "net" depending primarily upon whether adjustment is made for the latent heat of vaporization of the combustion products.

Hedging   Strategies to protect against financial loss resulting from an unfavorable price change, by locking in or containing the price of a future transaction. Hedging strategies for commodities include the purchase and sale of futures contracts and other derivatives.

Hertz (Hz)   The international standard unit of frequency, defined as the frequency of a periodic phenomenon with a period of one second. Electricity is generally either 50 Hz or 60 Hz.

High-voltage system   An electric power system having a maximum root-mean-square ac voltage above 72.5 kilovolts.

Horizontal drilling   Drilling of well bores that begin nearly vertically at the surface but which bend with depth until a significant segment, sometimes thousands of feet in length, diverges from the vertical by as much or more than 90°, becoming parallel to the earth's surface. While this practice is more costly per foot of well bore, it can dramatically reduce the unit cost of production by minimizing the number of separate wells needed and by exposing long, lateral sections of the well bore to the reservoir.

Hubs   A set of nearby interconnections between two or more pipelines and/or local distribution company main lines, and sometimes storage facilities, configured and operated to facilitate arms-length sales and purchases.

Hydrocarbon   An organic chemical compound of hydrogen and carbon in either gaseous, liquid, or solid phase. The molecular structure of hydrocarbon compounds varies from the simple, such as methane, to the very heavy and very complex.

I

Independent power producer (IPP)   A company that generates power but is not affiliated with an electric utility.

Induced current   Current in a conductor due to the application of a time-varying electromagnetic field.

Induced voltage   A voltage produced around a closed path or circuit by a change in magnetic flux linking that path.

Industrial market   Companies that buy products or services for business or trade use.

Industrial sector   Electric utilities generally divide customers into classes broadly, residential, commercial and industrial. The industrial sector includes manufacturing, construction, mining, agriculture and others. Industrial users generally have heavier electrical use than residential or commercial users.

Insulator   A material that is a very poor conductor of electricity. The insulating material is usually ceramic or fiberglass when used in an electric line and is designed to support a conductor physically and to separate it electrically from other conductors and supporting material.

Integrated resource planning   The process many utility commissions use to select the generation resources needed to meet future demand for electricity.

Intermediate load   In an electric system, intermediate load refers to the range from base load to a point between base load and peak load. This particular stage may be the mid-point, a percent of the peak load, or the load over a specified time period.

Internal combustion plant   A plant in which the prime mover is an internal combustion engine. This type of engine has one or more cylinders, in which the process of combustion takes place, converting energy released from the rapid burning of a fuel-air mixture into mechanical energy. Diesel or gasoline engines are the principal types used in electric plants. These plants are generally used only during periods of high electricity demand.

Interruptible gas   Gas sold to customers with a provision that permits curtailment or cessation of service at the discretion of the distributing company under certain circumstances, as specified in the service contract.

Interruptible load   Refers to program activities that, in accordance with contractual arrangements, can interrupt consumer load at times of seasonal peak load by direct control of the utility system operator or by action of the consumer at the direct request of the system operator. It usually involves commercial and industrial consumers.

Interruptible service   Sales and transportation service that is offered at both a lower cost and lower level of reliability. Under this service, gas companies can interrupt customers on short notice, typically during peak service days in the winter. Interruptible services are provided through individually negotiated contracts and, in most cases, the price and availability charged take into account the price of the customer's alternative fuel.

Investor-owned utility (IOU) Electric utilities organized as tax-paying businesses and generally financed by the sale of securities. The properties are managed by shareholder-elected representatives. These are usually set up as publicly owned corporations.

J

Joule A measurement of energy. It is the work done by a force of one Newton, when the point at which the force is applied is displaced one meter in the direction of the force. It is equal to 0.239 calories. In electrical theory, one joule equals one watt-second.

K

Kerosene A middle distillate, heavier than naphtha, refined from crude oil. It was an important illuminant before electric lighting became available, and today it is used for diesel fuels, home heating oil, and certain grades of jet fuels.

Kilovolt (kV) Equal to 1,000 volts.

Kilowatt hour (kWh) A measure for energy that is equal to the amount of work done by 1,000 watts for one hour. Consumers are charged for electricity in cents per kilowatt hour. With one kilowatt hour, you can watch television for about three hours.

Kilowatt (kW) A measurement of electric power equal to one thousand watts. Electric power capacity of one kW is sufficient to light ten, 100 watt light bulbs.

L

Lag The delay between two events.

Lift To bring oil or gas from a reservoir to the surface. Also, the natural fluid pressures that drive hydrocarbons to the surface.

Liquidity   The efficiency, including ease, speed, and economy, with which goods can be bought or sold.

Liquefied natural gas   Methane that is chilled below its boiling point so it can be stored in liquid form, thereby occupying 1/625 of the space it requires at ambient temperatures and pressures.

Load   The amount of electric power required at a given time by energy consumers which can be divided into three major classes—industrial load, commercial load, and residential load.

Local distribution company (LDC)   A utility that owns and operates a natural gas distribution system for the delivery of gas supplies from interstate pipelines at the city gate to the customer.

Lumen   The measuring unit of light flux.

Lux   The standard unit of illuminance. One lux is equal to one lumen per square meter.

M

Manufactured gas   Energy-rich vapors produced from controlled thermal decomposition or distillation of hydrocarbon feedstocks, including coal, oil, and coke-oven feedstocks. Manufactured gas historically had a low heating content. In the late 1970s and 1980s, however, the U.S. Department of Energy promoted construction of facilities to manufacture high-Btu synthetic natural gas suitable for commingling with natural gas in transmission pipelines.

Market-clearing price   The price at which supply and demand are in balance with respect to a particular commodity at a particular time. A market-clearing price is high enough to prevent a shortage but low enough to ensure that all supplies then available can be sold.

Marginal cost   The cost to increase output by one unit, such as the cost to produce one additional kWh of electricity.

Marginal revenue   Change in total revenue from the sale of one additional product or unit.

Maximum demand The greatest of all demands of the load that has occurred within a specified period of time.

Mcf One thousand cubic feet One Mcf of natural gas has a heating value of approximately one million Btu, also written MMBtu.

Megawatt (MW) One million watts.

Megawatt-hour (MWh) One million watts for one hour.

Merchant plant An electricity generating facility built and operated without long-term contracts guaranteeing sale of the electricity generated. Many such facilities are partial merchant plants, with contracts guaranteeing sale of a certain percentage of generation to a nearby utility.

Methane The simplest, lightest gaseous hydrocarbon, it is the primary component of natural gas.

Methanol The simplest of the alcohols. It is usually manufactured from methane.

Monopoly The exclusive control of a commodity or service by one entity. In the gas industry, interstate pipelines and local distribution companies are generally monopolies. Electricity has traditionally been operated as a local monopoly. Even after deregulation, it is anticipated that transmission infrastructure will remain regulated monopolies.

Municipal utility An electric utility system owned and/or operated by a municipality that generates and/or purchases electricity at wholesale for distribution to retail customers generally within the boundaries of the municipality.

N

Naphtha One of the lighter crude-oil fractions, from which gasoline products are blended. Naphtha was the dominant feedstock for oil-gas forms of manufactured gas and it is still used as feedstock for peak-shaving plants that produce substitute natural gas.

Natural gas A naturally occurring mixture of hydrocarbon and nonhydrocarbon gases found in porous geological formations beneath the earth's surface, often in association with petroleum. The principal constituent is methane.

Natural gas liquids (NGL)   Hydrocarbon components of wet gas whose molecules are larger than methane but smaller than crude oil. Gas liquids include ethane, propane, and butane.

Net capability   The maximum load-carrying ability of the equipment, exclusive of station use, under specified conditions for a given time interval, independent of the characteristics of the load. Capability is determined by design characteristics, physical conditions, prime mover, energy supply, and operating limitations, such as cooling and circulating water supply and temperature, headwater and tailwater elevations, and electrical use.

Net generation   Gross generation less the electric energy consumed at the generating stations for station use.

Net summer capability   The steady hourly output, which generating equipment is expected to supply to system load exclusive of auxiliary power, as demonstrated by tests at the time of summer peak demand.

Net winter capability   The steady hourly output which generating equipment is expected to supply to system load exclusive of auxiliary power, as demonstrated by tests at the time of winter peak demand.

NGA   The Natural Gas Act of 1938.

NGPA   The Natural Gas Policy Act of 1978.

Niche   A small slice of a broad market.

Non-associated gas   Natural gas from a reservoir that does not contain crude oil.

Nonattainment area   A geographic region in the U.S. designated by the Environmental Protection Agency as having ambient air concentrations of one or more criteria pollutants that exceed National Ambient Air Quality Standards.

Noncoincidental peak load   The sum of two or more peakloads on individual systems that do not occur in the same time interval. Meaningful only when considering loads within a limited period of time, such as a day, week, month, a heating or cooling season, and usually for not more than one year.

Non-firm power   Power or power-producing capacity supplied or available under a commitment having limited or no assured availability.

Nonutility generator (NUG)   A facility that produces electric power and sells it to an electric utility, usually under long-term contract. NUGs also tend to sell thermal energy and electricity to a nearby industrial customer.

Nonutility power producer   A corporation, person, agency, authority, or other legal entity that owns electric generating capacity and is not an electric utility. Nonutility power producers include qualifying small power producers and cogenerators without a designated franchised service territory.

North American Electric Reliability Council (NERC)   Electric utilities formed NERC to coordinate, promote, and communicate about the reliability of their generation and transmission systems. NERC reviews the overall reliability of existing and planned generation systems, sets reliability standards, and gathers data on demand, availability and performance.

O

Off-Peak Gas   Gas that is to be delivered and taken on demand when demand is not at its peak.

Off-peak power   Power supplied during designated periods of relatively low system demands.

Ohm   The unit of measurement of electrical resistance. Specifically, an ohm is the resistance of a circuit in which a potential difference of one volt produces a current of one ampere.

Ohmmeter   An instrument for measuring electric resistance.

Oil gas   Manufactured gas based on naphtha feedstocks.

Open access   Access to the commodity market via unbundled transmission capacity, for producers, end users, local distribution companies, and other gas resellers, on substantially equal terms for all kinds of shippers.

Operator   The legal entity, usually a working interest owner, responsible for the management and day-to-day operation of a well or lease.

Options   Financial derivatives that convey a right, but not an obligation, to buy or sell an underlying asset at a specified price until some fixed deadline, at which time the right expires.

Outage   The period during which a generating unit, transmission line, or other facility if out of service.

Over-the-counter   Pertaining to a financial asset or commodity, bought and sold away from an organized exchange, and thus an asset over which parties negotiate and conduct transactions directly between themselves.

Ozone transport   Ozone transport occurs when emissions from one area drift downwind and mix with local emissions contributing to the ozone concentrations in the downwind area.

Ozone   A compound consisting of three oxygen atoms. It is the primary constituent of smog.

P

Peak days   In electricity, the days in the summer months when the demand for electricity is at its highest level due to air conditioning load. For natural gas, peak days are the days in the winter months when demand for gas is at its highest level due to most heating equipment being used.

Peak load plant   A plant usually housing old, low-efficiency steam units, gas turbines, diesels, or pumped-storage hydroelectric equipment normally used during the peak load periods.

Peaking capacity   Capacity of generating equipment normally reserved for operation during the hours of highest daily, weekly, or seasonal loads. Some generating equipment may be operated at certain times as peaking capacity and at other times to serve loads on an around-the-clock basis.

Petroleum   Broadly, all naturally-occurring fluid hydrocarbons, including natural gas, condensate, crude oil, bitumens, and their respective fractions. Narrowly, liquid hydrocarbons, including crude oil and the liquid products of refining crude oil.

pH   A measure of the acidity or alkalinity of a material, liquid, or solid.

Pipeline   All physical equipment through which gas is moved in transportation, including pipes, valves, and other attachments.

Pipeline quality gas Natural gas within 5% of the heating value of pure methane, or 1,010 Btu per cubic foot under standard atmospheric conditions, and free of water and toxic or corrosive contaminants.

Plant-use electricity The electric energy used in the operation of a plant. This energy total is subtracted from the gross energy production of the plant. For reporting purposes the plant energy production is then reported as a net figure. The energy required for pumping at pumped-storage plants is, by definition, subtracted, and the energy production for these plants is then reported as a net figure.

Poolco A market structure that some have proposed for the electric industry. With Poolcos, a central authority would purchase all power from generating companies and resell it to distribution utilities. There are no Poolcos in the U.S.

Power marketer A company that buys and resells power. These merchants typically do not own generating facilities.

Power pools A group of utilities that coordinate the operation of their power plants and share the costs between themselves. Power pools are especially common in the northeastern U.S.

Power surge A sudden change in an electrical system's voltage that is capable of damaging electrical equipment.

Power The instantaneous current being delivered at a given voltage, measured in watts, or more usually kilowatts. Power delivered for a period of time is energy, measured in kilowatt-hours.

Primary energy A statistical category of marketed energy, confined to supplies that are not derived from another marketed energy form. For example, electricity generated from fossil fuels is not a primary energy source because it comes from gas, oil, or coal.

Prime mover The engine, turbine, water wheel, or similar machine that drives an electrical generator. Generally, a prime mover refers to a device that converts energy to electricity directly, such as photovoltaic solar and fuel cells.

Private power producer   Any entity that engages in wholesale power generation or in self-generation.

Privatization   Conversion of a government-owned firm or industry to private ownership.

Producing capacity   The maximum rate at which a field or some other producing unit can flow hydrocarbons through existing surface equipment without causing damage to the productive reservoir.

Producing sector   The part of the gas industry that finds hydrocarbons, conveys them from the reservoir to the surface, and delivers them to a buyer in a first sale.

Propane   A hydrocarbon component of produced natural gas. It is one of the natural gas liquids, also an oil-refinery byproduct and the principal constituent of liquefied petroleum gas.

Public utility   Publicly owned electric utilities are nonprofit local government agencies established to serve their communities and nearby consumers at cost, returning excess funds to the consumer in the form of community contributions, economic and efficient facilities, and lower rates. Publicly owned electric utilities number approximately 2,000 in the U.S., and include municipals, public power districts, state authorities, irrigation districts, and others.

Public utility commission (PUC)   An administrative or quasi-judicial body at the state provincial or municipal level, whose functions include regulation of public utilities.

Public Utility Holding Company Act of 1935 (PUHCA)   PUHCA regulates the large interstate holding companies that monopolized the electric utility industry in the early part of the twentieth century.

Purchased power adjustment   A clause in a rate schedule that provides for adjustments to the bill when energy from another electric system is acquired and it varies from a specified unit base amount.

Public Utility Regulatory Policies Act of 1978 (PURPA)   PURPA promotes energy efficiency and increased use of alternative energy sources, encouraging companies to build cogeneration facilities and renewable energy projects. Facilities meeting PURPA's requirements are called qualifying facilities or QFs.

Q

Quad Abbreviation for one quadrillion Btu. For natural gas, this is roughly one trillion cubic feet.

Qualifying facility (QF) A generator that 1) qualifies as a cogenerator or small power producer under PURPA and 2) has obtained certification from FERC. They generally sell power to utilities at the utilities' avoided cost.

R

Rate base The value of property upon which a utility is permitted to earn a specified rate of return as established by a regulatory authority. The rate base generally represents the value of property used by the utility in providing service and may be calculated by any one or a combination of the following accounting methods: fair value, prudent investment, reproduction cost, or original cost. Depending on which method is used, the rate base includes cash, working capital, materials and supplies, and deductions for accumulated provisions for depreciation, contributions in aid of construction, customer advances for construction, accumulated deferred income taxes, and accumulated deferred investment tax credits.

Raw gas Natural gas as it issues from the reservoir, including mainly methane and possibly heavier hydrocarbons, as well as impurities such as hydrogen sulfide, carbon dioxide, and water.

Recovery rate The fraction of the original oil or gas in place deemed to be recoverable with current technology. Alternatively the fraction of original oil or gas in place projected to be recovered with installed or firmly planned field equipment.

Regional transmission group A voluntary organization of transmission owners, transmission users, and other entities approved by the Federal Energy Regulatory Commission to efficiently coordinate transmission planning and expansion, operation, and use on a regional basis.

Regulating transformer A transformer used to vary the voltage, or the phase angle, or both, of an output circuit controlling the output within specified limits, and compensating for fluctuations of load and input voltage.

Regulation The government function of controlling or directing economic entities through the process of rulemaking and adjudication.

Regulator An electrical device that raises or lowers the voltage of the circuit to which it is attached.

Regulatory compact A theory advocated by some utilities which holds that in exchange for building the generation, transmission, and distribution infrastructure necessary to provide power to their service area, the utility is guaranteed a return on those investments.

Regulatory environment Regulations and enforcement affecting marketing activities that are laid down by government and non-government entities.

Reliability council A group of interconnected utilities in a geographical area that work together to assure system-wide reliability.

Renewable energy Refers to any source of energy that is constantly replenished through natural processes. Sunlight, moving water, geothermal springs, biomass, and wind are all examples of renewable energy resources used to generate electricity.

Reserve margin (Operating) The amount of unused available capability of an electric power system at peakload for a utility system as a percentage of total capability.

Reserves With respect to oil or gas, that part of the resource that is commercially recoverable under current economic conditions with current technology. "Proved" reserves are the portion of the resource that is in known reservoirs and believed to be recoverable with the highest degree of confidence. "Indicated" or "probable" reserves are the additional resources associated with known reservoirs that are expected to be recoverable. "Speculative" reserves are those resources, in addition to the others already mentioned, outside the vicinity of known reservoirs, which are expected to be recoverable.

Reserves-to-production (R/P ratio) For a particular gas field or fields, the ratio of remaining recoverable reserves to the current annual rate of production.

Residential The residential sector is defined as private household establishments which consume energy primarily for space heating, water heating, air conditioning, lighting, refrigeration, cooking and clothes drying. The classification of an individual consumer's account, where the use is both residential and commercial, is based on principal use. For the residential class, do not duplicate consumer accounts due to multiple metering for special services (water, heating, etc). Apartment houses are also included.

Residual oil The heavier hydrocarbons contained in crude oil, which do not boil off in the distillation process.

Residue gas Natural gas after treatment to remove impurities and processing to extract liquids, but before adjustment to bring heating value to the pipeline quality range.

Restructuring The process of separating, or unbundling, the true monopoly functions of a local natural gas utility—such as the physical delivery, or distribution of natural gas to a home or business through pipelines—from those services—such as providing natural gas supply—that can be offered competitively.

Retail wheeling The transmission of power to an individual customer from a generator of electricity other than the host utility. The National Energy Policy Act, enacted in 1992, prohibits the Federal Energy Regulatory Commission from mandating retail wheeling. States and their regulatory bodies, however, are free to enact their own retail wheeling initiatives.

Retail Sales covering electrical energy supplied for residential, commercial, and industrial end-use purposes. Other small classes, such as agriculture and street lighting, also are included in this category.

Retrofit To change an existing piece of equipment or facility in order to improve its performance or efficiency.

Running and quick-start capability The net capability of generating units that carry load or have quick-start capability. In general, quick-start capability refers to generating units that can be available for load within a 30-minute period.

Rural Electric Cooperatives (REC) Organizations composed of rural customers that band together to generate or purchase power at wholesale rates and then distribute it at retail rates.

Rural Electrification Administration (REA) This agency was formed in 1936 to provide low-interest loans to expand electric service to rural areas.

S

Sales for resale Energy supplied to other electric utilities, cooperatives, municipalities, and federal and state electric agencies for resale to ultimate consumers.

Scheduled outage The shutdown of a generating unit, transmission line, or other facility, for inspection or maintenance, in accordance with an advance schedule.

Secondary markets Resale markets for goods whose first-sale prices and/or allocation are constrained by long-term contracts, monopoly power, or government regulation. Unconstrained secondary-market transactions can reallocate goods to their highest value uses, mitigate or even eliminate shortages and surpluses caused by price controls, and thus substantially improve the efficiency of resource allocation.

Sedimentary basins Large geographic areas that contain rock strata of a sedimentary nature, deposited when the topography was conducive to sedimentation, as in lakes or shallow seas.

Seismic survey A method of geophysical exploration that creates visual representations of the subsurface from reflection of sound waves off boundaries between rock layers of different density.

Self-regulation Industry activities and efforts to police itself.

Service territory The geographical area served by a particular utility company.

Short circuit   An abnormal connection of relatively low impedance, whether made accidentally or intentionally, between two points of different potential in a circuit.

Small power producer   Under the Public Utility Regulatory Policies Act (PURPA), a small power production facility or small power producer generates electricity using waste, renewable, or geothermal energy as a primary energy source. Fossil fuels can be used, but renewable resources must provide at least 75% of the total energy input.

Spinning reserve   That reserve generating capacity running at a zero load and synchronized to the electric system.

Spot market transaction   Commodity sale/purchase transactions whereby participants' buy and sell commitments are of short duration at a single volumetric price, relative to term or contract markets in which transactions are long-term and pricing provisions are often complex. For natural gas, spot transactions typically have durations of one month or less.

Standby facility   A facility that supports a utility system and is generally running under no-load. It is available to replace or supplement a facility normally in service.

Standby service   Support service that is available, as needed, to supplement a consumer, a utility system, or to another utility if a schedule or an agreement authorizes the transaction. The service is not regularly used.

Steam electric plant   A plant in which the prime mover is a steam turbine. The steam used to drive the turbine is produced in a boiler where fossil fuels are burned.

Stranded benefits   Social programs and other regulatory "benefits" currently included in utility rates that could be stranded in an open market.

Stranded costs   This refers to a utility's fixed costs, usually related to investments in generation facilities, that would no longer be paid by customers through their rates in the event that they opt to purchase power from other suppliers.

Stranded costs/investment   Utility assets, mainly high-cost power plants, that would lose value in a competitive market.

Structural unbundling See vertical disaggregation.

Substation Facility equipment that switches, changes, or regulates electric voltage.

Swaps Over-the-counter financial derivatives in which a buyer and seller of a physical commodity or financial asset exchange cash flows from physical transactions. They make or receive periodic payments to or from one another based on the difference between physical market realizations and a specified index price.

Switchgear A general term covering switching and interrupting devices and their combination with associated control, metering, protective and regulating devices, also assemblies of these devices with associated interconnection, accessories, enclosures and supporting structure used primarily in connection with the generation, transmission, distribution, and conversion of electric power.

Switching station Facility equipment used to tie together two or more electric circuits through switches. The switches are selectively arranged to permit a circuit to be disconnected, or to change the electric connection between the circuits.

T

Take-or-pay A contractual obligation to pay for a certain threshold quantity of gas whether or not the buyer finds it possible to take timely full delivery. Typically, the buyer still retains a right to take the volumes for which it has prepaid, but only after taking all the volumes it had a subsequent obligation to buy.

Tariff A list of terms, conditions, and rate information applied to various types of gas service. These tariffs are filed and approved by the Federal Energy Regulatory Commission or the state regulator.

Therm One therm equals 100,000 Btu.

Time-of-day pricing A rate structure that prices electricity at different rates, reflecting the changes in the utility's costs of providing electricity at different times of the day.

Tolling An arrangement whereby a party moves fuel to a power generator and receives kilowatt hours in return for a pre-established fee.

Transformer An electrical device for changing the voltage of alternating current.

Transmission circuit A conductor used to transport electricity from generating stations to load.

Transmission company A company engaged solely in the transmission function of the electric power industry.

Transmission grid The high voltage wires that connect generation facilities with distribution facilities. It is the infrastructure through which power moves around the U.S. It is necessary to carefully coordinate use of the transmission system to ensure reliable and efficient service.

Transmission line A set of conductors, insulators, supporting structures, and associated equipment used to move large quantities of power at high voltage.

Transmission system An interconnected group of electric transmission lines and associated equipment for moving or transferring electric energy in bulk between points of supply and points at which it is transformed for delivery over the distribution lines to consumers or is delivered to other electric systems.

Transmission The movement or transfer of electric energy over an interconnected group of lines and associated equipment between points of supply and points at which it is transformed for delivery to consumers, or is delivered to other electric systems. Transmission is considered to end when the energy is transformed for distribution to the consumer. Also, in natural gas, the conveyance of natural gas from producing to consuming areas through large-diameter, high-pressure pipelines.

Transportation Service in which a gas pipeline or distribution company moves gas owned by others from one location to another for a fee.

Turbine A machine for generating rotary mechanical power from the energy of a stream of fluid (such as water, steam, or hot gas). Turbines convert the kinetic energy of fluids to mechanical energy through the principles of impulse and reaction, or a mixture of the two.

U

Ultra-high voltage systems   Electric systems in which the operating voltage levels have a maximum root-mean-square ac voltage above 800,000 volts (800 kV).

Unbundling   The process of separating natural gas services into components with each component priced separately. Traditionally, numerous gas services, such as sales, local transportation, and storage, had been tied together and offered to customers as a single, bundled product. By separating services into components, unbundling enables customers to compare the value of each service to its price. Unbundling also allows customers to choose those individual services that meet their own energy needs. This practice is expected to be part of the deregulation of the electric industry as well with generation, transmission, and distribution segments separated, as well as various value-added services and ancillary services.

Usage rates   Segmenting consumers according to the volume of product they buy and the speed at which they use it.

Useful thermal output   The thermal energy made available for use in any industrial or commercial process, or used in any heating or cooling application, i.e., total thermal energy made available for processes and applications other than electrical generation.

Utility   Privately owned companies and public agencies engaged in the generation, transmission, or distribution of electric power for public use.

V

Value-added services   Services, such as security monitoring, telecommunications, internet access, and others, that add value to electric services. Other services which can be offered by utilities to achieve greater customer satisfaction and loyalty.

Variable costs   Those costs borne by electric utilities that vary with the level of electric output and include fuel expenses.

Vertical disaggregation   Separating electric generation, transmission, and distribution functions of a utility into separate companies.

Vertically integrated utility   Utilities that sell power on a bundled basis and whose activities run the full range of different functional activities of generation, transmission, and distribution. With deregulation of the electric utility industry well under way, vertically integrated electric utilities may well be on their way out.

Volt   The measure of pressure that pushes electric current through a circuit.

Volt-Ampere, reactive (VAR)   A reactive load, typically inductive from electric motors, which causes more current to flow in the distribution network than is actually consumed by the load. This requires excess capability on the generation side and causes greater power losses in the distribution network.

Voltmeter   An instrument that measures the electric potential difference between two points in a circuit in volts.

W

Watt   The basic expression of electrical power or the rate of electrical work. One watt is the power resulting from the dissipation of one joule of energy in one second.

Watt-hour   An electrical energy unit of measure equal to one watt of power supplied to, or taken from, an electric circuit steadily for one hour.

Wellhead price   The price or value in the first sale of oil or gas, for regulatory, royalty, or tax purposes. This first sale may actually take place at the well, the lease or unit boundary, the tailgate of a gas-processing plant, or the intake flange of a pipeline.

Wheeling service   The movement of electricity from one system to another over transmission facilities of intervening systems. Wheeling service contracts can be established between two or more systems.

Wheeling   The transportation of power to customers. Wholesale wheeling is transmitting bulk power over the grid to power companies. Retail

wheeling is transmitting power to end users, such as homes, businesses, and factories.

Wholesale wheeling   The use of transmission facilities of one system to
transmit power by agreement of and for another system with a corresponding wheeling charge Wholesale wheeling involves only sales for
resale and occurs when the buyer of the power resells the wheeled
power to retail customers.

Appendix B
Convergence/
Btu Industry Contacts

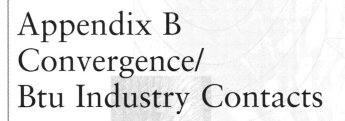

Alternative Fuels Data Center
P.O. Box 12316
Arlington, VA 22209
(800) 423-1363

American Gas Association
1515 Wilson Boulevard
Arlington, VA 22209
(703) 841-8400

American Nuclear Society
555 North Kensington Avenue
La Grange Park, IL 60526
(708) 352-6611

American Petroleum Institute
1220 L Street, NW
Washington, DC 20005
(202) 682-8000

American Public Gas Association

11094-D Lee Hwy., Suite 102

Fairfax, VA 22030

(703) 352-3890

American Public Power Association

2301 M Street, NW

Washington, DC 20036

(202) 775-8300

American Solar Energy Society

2400 Central Avenue, Suite G-1

Boulder, CO 80301

(303) 443-3130

American Wind Energy Association

122 C Street, NW, 4th Floor

Washington, D.C. 20001

(202) 383-2500

ASME International

345 E. 47th Street

New York, N.Y. 10017-2392

(212) 705-7722

Association of Edison Illuminating Companies

600 N. 18th Street

Birmingham, AL 35291-0992

(205) 250-2530

Association of Energy Engineers

4025 Pleasantdale Road, Suite 420

Atlanta, GA 30340-4264

(770) 447-5083

Association of Northwest Gas Utilities

34 NW First Ave., Suite 209

Portland, OR 97209

(503) 228-4754

Bonneville Power Administration

P.O. Box 362

Portland, OR 97208

(503) 230-3000

Compressed Gas Association

1725 Jefferson Davis Highway, Suite 1004

Arlington, VA 22202

(703) 412-0900

Council On Environmental Quality

722 Jackson Place, NW

Washington, DC 20503

(202) 395-5750

Department of Commerce

14th Street & Constitution Avenue, SW

Washington, D.C. 20230

(202) 482-2112

Department of Energy, U.S.

1000 Independent Avenue, SW

Washington, D.C. 20585

(202) 622-2000

Edison Electric Institute

701 Pennsylvania Avenue, NW

Washington, DC 20004-2696

(202) 508-5000

Electric Generation Association

1401 H Street, NW, Suite 760

Washington, D.C. 20005

(202) 789-7200

Electrical Generating Association

2101 L Street, NW, Suite 405

Washington, D.C. 20037

(202) 965-1134

Electric Power Supply Association

1401 H Street, NW, Suite 760

Washington, DC 20005

(202) 789-7200

Electric Power Research Institute

3412 Hillview Avenue

Palo Alto, CA 94304

(415) 855-2000

Energy Information Administration

Forrestal Building, Room 1F-048

Washington, D.C. 20585

(202) 586-8800

Environmental Protection Agency

401 M Street, SW

Washington, D.C. 20460

(202) 260-2090

Federal Emergency Management Agency

Federal Center Plaza

500 C Street, SW

Washington, D.C. 20571

(202) 646-2500

Federal Energy Regulatory Commission

888 First Street, NE

Washington, D.C. 20426

(202) 208-0200

Gas Appliance Manufacturers Association

1901N. Moore Street

Arlington, VA 22209

(703) 525-9565

Gas Processors Association

6526 East 60th Street

Box 35584 (74153)

Tulsa, OK 74145

(918) 493-3872

Geothermal Resources Council

2001 2nd Street, Box 1350

Davis, CA 95617

(916) 758-2360

Independent Petroleum Association of America

1101 16th Street NW

Washington, DC 20036

(202) 857-4722

INGAA

555 13th Street NW, Suite 300 West

Washington, DC 20004

(202) 626-3200

Institute of Electrical and Electronics Engineers, Inc.

345 E. 47th Street

New York, NY 10017-2394

(212) 705-7900

Institute of Nuclear Power Operations

700 Galleria Parkway

Atlanta, GA 30339-5957

(770) 644-8000

International District Energy Association

1200 19th Street, NW, Suite 300

Washington, D.C. 20036-2422

(202) 429-5111

Interstate Oil and Gas Compact Commission

900 Northeast 23rd Street

Oklahoma City, OK 73105

(405) 525-3556

Midwest Gas Association

7831 Glenroy Rd., Suite 300

Minneapolis, MN 55435

(612) 832 9915

National Association of Regulatory Utility Commissioners

1102 I.C.C. Building

P.O. Box 684

Washington, D.C. 20044

(202) 898-2200

National Bioenergy Industries Association

122 C Street, NW, 4th Floor

Washington, D.C. 20001

(202) 383-2540

National Electrical Manufacturers Association

1300 N. 17th Street, Suite 1847

Rosslyn, VA 22209

(703) 841-3200

National Energy Information Center

1000 Independence Avenue, SW

Washington, D.C. 20585

(202) 586-8800

National Independent Energy Producers

601 13th Street, NW, Suite 320 South

Washington, D.C. 20005

(202) 793-6506

National Hydropower Association

122 C Street, NW, 4th Floor

Washington, D.C. 20001

(202) 383-2530

National Mining Association

1130 17th Street, NW

Washington, D.C. 20036

(202) 463-2625

National Renewable Energy Laboratory

1617 Cole Boulevard

Golden, CO 80401

(303) 275-3000

National Rural Electric Cooperative Association

4301 Wilson Boulevard

Arlington, VA 22203

(703) 907-5500

National Science Foundation

4201 Wilson Boulevard

Arlington, VA 22203

(703) 306-1224

Natural Gas Association of Houston

1221 Lamar Road, Suite 630

Houston, TX 77010

(713) 651-0551

Natural Gas Supply Association

805 15th Street NW

Washington, DC 20005

(202) 326-9300

Natural Gas Vehicle Coalition

1515 Wilson Boulevard, Suite 1030

Arlington, VA 22209

(703) 527-3022

The New England Gas Association

75 Second Avenue, Suite 510

Needham Heights, MA 02494-2800

(781) 455-6800

North American Electric Reliability Council

Princeton Forrestal Village

116-390 Village Boulevard

Princeton, NJ 08540-5731

(609) 452-8060

Nuclear Energy Institute

1776 I Street, NW, Suite 400

Washington, D.C. 20006-3708

(202) 739-8075

Nuclear Regulatory Commission

Washington, D.C. 20555

(301) 622-7000

Occupational Safety & Health Administration

200 Constitution Avenue, NW, Room S2315

Washington, D.C. 20210

(202) 219-6091

Pacific Coast Gas Association

1350 Bayshore Highway, Suite 340

Burlingame, CA 94010

(415) 579-7000

Rocky Mountain Gas Association

2170 S. Parker Road, Suite 215

Denver, CO 80231

(303) 338-1472

Rural Utility Service

South Agriculture Building, 14th & Independence

AG Box 1532, SW

Washington, D.C. 20250-1500

(202) 720-9560

Solar Energy Industries Association

122 C Street, NW, 4th Floor

Washington, D.C. 20001-2109

(202) 383-2600

Southeastern Gas Association

PO Box 247

Willow Springs, NC 27592

(919) 552-6521

Southeastern Power Administration

Samual Elbert Building, 2 S. Public Square

Elberton, GA 30635

(706) 213-3800

Southern Gas Association

3030 LBJ Freeway, Suite 1300, LB 60

Dallas, TX 75234

(214) 387-8505

Southwestern Power Administration

P.O. Box 1619

Tulsa, OK 74101

(918) 581-7474

Tennessee Valley Authority

400 W. Summitt Hill Drive

Knoxville, TN 37902-1499

(615) 632-2101

Texas Independent Producers and Royalty Owners Association

515 Congress Avenue, Suite 1910

Austin, TX 78701

(512) 477-4452

Western Area Power Administration

P.O. Box 3402

Golden, CO 80401-3398

(303) 231-1513

United States Energy Association

1620 Eye Street, NW, Suite 1000

Washington, D.C. 20006

(202) 331-0415

UTC, Telecommunications Association

1140 Connecticut Avenue, NW, Suite 1140

Washington, D.C. 20036

(202) 872-0031

Index

A

F

H

N

O

P

S